FATHERS and DAUGHTERS

WILLIAM S. APPLETON, M.D.

FATHERS and DAUGHTERS

A Father's Powerful Influence
on a Woman's Life

Doubleday & Company, Inc., Garden City, New York

Library of Congress Cataloging in Publication Data

Appleton, William S.
Fathers and daughters.

1. Fathers and daughters.   I. Title.
HQ756.A66   306.8'7
ISBN 0-385-15511-5   AACR2
Library of Congress Catalog Card Number 80-1649

For my daughters, Amy and Lucy,
and my son, Bill.
And to my father.

Contents

Introduction

In twenty years as a psychiatrist I have listened to hundreds
of sensitive and intelligent women tell me of disappointments
with their careers and in their relationships with men. Because of my monthly column in *Cosmopolitan* magazine I receive hundreds of letters from women describing problems
with lovers. I have been surprised at how rare it is in this
Freudian age that any of these troubled daughters identify
their fathers as a contributing factor in their adult unhappiness. I decided to interview eighty-one women, outside my
practice, in great depth and to focus on the effect of their
male parents on their adult lives. I selected them at random,
based on their willingness to be interviewed, from classes and
seminars I taught, social gatherings I attended, and places
where I work and consult. Most women are very willing to
discuss their fathers' effect on them.

What I found was very interesting. Of course their fathers'

legacy deeply colors their careers and private lives. I wondered why my patients and my *Cosmopolitan* readers had not told me, of their own accord, what all women know, that their years with their fathers leave a profound mark. From them I discovered that they did realize the importance of paternal influence but saw no application for the knowledge. Consequently they had no reason to volunteer observations about their fathers. A pattern emerges. When queried, young women often reported an inability to sustain intimacy, enjoy success, and advance confidently in their careers. Questioned further they often described their fathers quite perceptively. Yet they failed to undo his negative influence from the past in order to overcome their present difficulties.

My purpose in writing this book is to help women change, alter unhappy love affairs, find more pleasure in sex, and realize full potential in their careers. Focusing on the father-daughter relationship will not magically produce all these results, but use of this knowledge in the way I suggest will help them reach some of these goals.

As I said, knowing that a father was unsupportive does not help a woman build confidence in her career or with lovers. Just "seeing" is not enough. The reason is twofold. The first involves a defense mechanism known as *isolation,* which enables an individual to detach an occurrence and keep it from becoming part of his or her significant experience. The incident is not forgotten but is deprived of its emotional content, and its associative connections are suppressed. That is why women "see" how their fathers influenced them but are unable to emotionally integrate the fact.

What surprised me was that overcoming this defense mechanism did not help as much as classical psychoanalysis suggested it should. The reason is that it represented only a part of the total problem between father and daughter. One forty-five-year-old woman, whom I will call Carol Jacobs, had spent her life furious at men; by overcoming the defense of isolation she was able to connect it to her hatred of her father for having deserted the family. However, only after she learned he was dying was she able to recall the childhood warmth and closeness they shared. Another woman, whom I will call Joan Taylor, described the arrogance of the men with whom she tried to become intimate. Once her defense of isolation subsided she was able to connect the source of her problem with lovers to her overpowering father. Only much later was she able to realize that it was his mind she most respected in the world and that her difficulty with men arose not from their authoritarian treatment but from the fact that none seemed as bright as her father or, by extension, as she. It was she who looked down on her lovers.

The second reason why a woman might fail to understand the connection between her relationship to her father and her adult difficulties is that her perception is too narrow and literal. What she thinks she comprehends she in fact does not.

To understand her father's influence a woman needs to begin with a full picture of him. In addition to overcoming repression and recovering her memories, she must broaden her view of the years with her male parent. When psychoanalytic theory was formulated, knowledge of the stages of adult development did not exist. A father, therefore, was conceived of as a simple, one-dimensional figure. The analytic patient's unconscious view of him was accepted as psychological reality. We now know people change throughout their adult lives. Fathers develop and so do daughters. The women who spoke first of hating their fathers and then of loving them were describing different times in their lives. At first Carol Jacobs could only remember being deserted by her father when she was eighteen; only later did she uncover the memories of his thoughtfulness and attention in her childhood.

None of these discoveries refuted the value of psychoanalysis for me. It simply confirmed that the relationship between fathers and daughters could best be understood in terms of two evolving life cycles, sometimes meshing and sometimes clashing.

For a woman to understand how her history with her father influences her capacity for a fulfilling career and emotional intimacy she must comprehend fully all their years together and the effect they have had. Once she understands the development of her own needs and how they color her choice of and behavior toward a man, she is then able to begin changing any patterns she finds painful and unsatisfying.

The reason why most women do not overcome any ill effects of their years with father is not due to repression of illicit sexual desires nearly so much as to the sheer enormity of understanding the changes in him and in themselves. The little girl saw one father, the adolescent a second, the adult a third. And often the father hid from her because he was shy, too busy, or trying to protect her from harsh realities. Even when he was available and candid she might not have been able or willing to understand because she was too young, too unrealistic, too afraid and angry, or too much in love with him.

A father plays many roles, including breadwinner, disciplinarian, authority, boyfriend, Santa Claus. A daughter observes him through her child's eyes and needs, sometimes realistically, often in a distorted way. Their years together are a time of growth and change for both. The process, I learned from my investigations, takes about thirty years. At the end, if it works well, a woman becomes mature and capable of warm sex, lasting intimacy, and a successful career.

Through my research I have learned it takes a woman until the age of thirty to completely understand her relationship to her father. By this time he is sixty, fully evolved and revealed. One may quibble with the arbitrary numbers, placing the daughter's coming of age into the twenties; also, significant changes can occur after the age of thirty and even after sixty. Yet on the average, if a woman understands her development with respect to her father up until the age of thirty, she will have enough information to help her in all facets of her life.

In order for a woman to comprehend thirty years with her father, she cannot be blinded by a singular emotional memory. Surely the woman filled with anger at her father's arrogance was correct in saying it affected her adult affairs, but she lacked the perspective necessary for seeing how her respect for his brilliance made her look down on men. Contemplating the whole picture and acknowledging her own arrogance enabled her to begin to get along better with men her own age.

Yet comprehension is not all. A daughter then faces the challenge of converting her intellectual knowledge to emotional knowledge and using it wisely to undo damages incurred in growing up. For example, one thirty-four-year-old woman told of a father who constantly gave orders, demanded and got obedience, and monopolized the thinking of all his family. She herself complained that men were arrogant and sought power over women. This, she soon realized, made her seek weak men she could dominate. She came to see how she enjoyed leading them and being like her father. Still later she understood how weak, indecisive, and incapable she felt compared to her father and men other than her lovers. Nor could she admire her ineffectual lovers. A woman's suffering often comes from an obscure chain like the one I have just described. It is hard for her to see the connection between her inner feelings and the way she lives. Only by understanding how the arrogant father of whom she initially complained had left her with a need she detested, a need to be ordered about, could this woman begin to change the way she lived and thus the way she felt.

It is suffering that motivates the desire for change. A succession of unhappy love affairs, inability to enjoy sex, feelings of insecurity, repeated failure in a career, these cause the pain that stimulates the wish to alter an unhappy pattern. But to do so one must recognize alternative ways to behave and feel the power to make a choice. However essential an instrument for change awareness is, it is not enough. Insight tells you where you are, how you got there, and where to go. In addition to it your own effort and will are necessary to change your life. The woman who believes herself intellectually superior to each of her lovers as her father was to her will not stop feeling this way by insight alone. She must begin to prefer intimacy and equality to domination and subjection. She should learn to enjoy a man as an equal, allowing herself to admire areas in which he is superior and accepting those in which he is not. Ultimately it is her responsibility if she wants to change her relationship to men. Others can act as a catalyst, giving comfort and encouragement, but only she can do it.

With this book, I hope to help women achieve insight into the complicated touching of two life cycles over thirty years. I have developed a scheme to enable them to do so quickly and completely. This will be revealed in the following chapters. Yet I feel it my duty to tell women now that the rest must come from them. Fundamental change requires a long time, years not months, and obstacles may at times appear overwhelming. A woman may be convinced there is no man as bright or kind as her father was. She is lonely yet unable to enjoy intimacy with a man. Her problem is connected to the effect her male parent had on her. Each effort to find a man of her own will require further insight. Sometimes her attempt to change the way she relates to lovers will require a new insight and sometimes action will have to come before knowledge. There is no easy way. But a determined woman armed with thorough knowledge of her father's effect on her has a good chance. The strength of her will, mind, and heart will make it possible for her to change.

FATHERS and DAUGHTERS

One

TWO LIFE CYCLES

The interplay of three facts continues to trouble me in my role as psychiatrist, psychiatric columnist for *Cosmopolitan* magazine, and father of two daughters. The first is the large number of women who are unhappy at work and in their private lives. The second is that in this age of psychology most of them think they understand their father's role in their adult dissatisfactions but in reality do not. And the third is how hard it is to understand and change unproductive patterns in their personal lives and in their careers.

The more a woman understands her father's effect and makes use of this knowledge, the more she will be able to enjoy her husband or lover sexually, emotionally, and intellectually, the freer she will be to pursue and advance in her career, the better she will be as a mother to her own children, and the richer her life will become.

I have chosen the first thirty years of a woman's life on

which to focus. This is not to say that the experience of a girl of eighteen is unimportant or that a fifty-year-old woman has learned nothing in twenty additional years. It is just that my clinical knowledge and research has convinced me that thirty years is a manageable way to look at the subject. The father is by then about sixty years old and stands fully revealed while the woman at thirty is mature. I am completely aware that ages thirty and sixty are by no means the end of growth, development, and change, but by this time the greatest influences have been exerted, and subsequent changes are slow and more difficult to affect.

UNDERSTANDING THIRTY YEARS BETWEEN YOU AND FATHER

There are three reasons why understanding thirty years is extremely difficult. It is hard to know yourself and many people take three to five years in analysis or therapy to try to do so. Gaining insight into your father over three decades is not easy either. There are thousands of experiences and emotions remembered and forgotten, ignored through habit or deeply unconscious, emotional attachments and longings of which a woman is unaware. And finally there is the interaction of the two of you and how it has grown, changed, and affected both you and him in deep and long-lasting ways.

There are three methods that can be used to understand the effect your father has had and continues to have on you. The first is used by every woman, especially those who are sensitive and psychologically minded. This is introspection. Just about every daughter has thought about how her father has influenced her, especially in her relationships to men. Introspection can be very revealing and effective in overcoming problems. But unfortunately, two things can block this effort: psychological defensiveness and the vastness of the subject. The first can be overcome by a psychoanalytically oriented technique in which defense mechanisms are removed, freeing the mind to remember and use the insights to effect growth and change. The second, the sheer volume of thirty years and a multitude of experiences, can be simplified and viewed in a more manageable way by a model I have developed to help women do so.

The Psychoanalytic Way

Psychoanalytic insight is gained by overcoming the following nine defense mechanisms: regression, repression, reaction formation, isolation, undoing, projection, introjection, turning against the self, and reversal. Of these, two seem to be most important in preventing the understanding of father's psychological impact on his daughter. The first, repression, is well known: it is the mental process by which an unacceptable impulse or idea is rendered unconscious. Repression is less important now than it was in Freud's time because of Freud's own influence and because of the abandonment of Victorian attitudes, which has made many ideas and impulses acceptable; there is no more need for the mind to repress them.

Isolation is a more important and less well known defense mechanism. The incident is not forgotten but deprived of its emotional and intellectual connections to the woman's life. An example of this would be provided by a daughter whose father was generous, loving, and supportive, and whose lovers are invariably old, rich, and kind, but whose knowledge of her paternal ties is emotionally unconnected to her behavior with her lovers. Many women are able to acknowledge how their bad relationships with men arise from ones they had with their fathers, but the full connection is not emotionally felt and the realization does not influence their behavior. Once the defense is chipped away and the woman begins to feel her helpless need for an older lover's fatherlike care, she is able to begin to abandon this pattern and enjoy men her own age.

After a woman overcomes the defense mechanisms of repression and isolation, the problem of liberating herself from her father's influence on her relationships with men remains very great. The reason is that for most women there is no one memory or answer to be recovered. The movie version of psychoanalysis in which this happens is unreal. There is no single force that governs a woman's life that can be made conscious and cure her. It would be nice if there were one simple answer to your problems with men—if all you had to do was work through the wish to sleep with your father and the complications and anguish you suffer with men ceased. The analyses Freud thought he could complete in six months have been found to require five years, and even then the father's adverse influence on his daughter is often unaltered. The dramatic effect of one repressed memory is no more simplistically illustrated than in Orson Welles' *Citizen Kane*, in which all of Kane's years of striving, acquiring, and collecting are boiled down to the loss of his childhood sled Rosebud. Perhaps this is merely a literary, filmic symbol; one should not take Welles to task, as one certainly cannot sum up Freudian theory as the desire of a girl to sleep with her father, but it is the very attitude of reducing complex psychological problems to one or a few causes which can prevent solutions. The technique and theory of psychoanalysis, therefore, is too focused on early childhood to help a woman fully understand the thirty years of interaction with her father and its effect on her. More than early childhood is involved.

Furthermore, the clinical method of free association, which Freud discovered, does not encourage a balanced thirty-year perspective. What "comes to mind" are the most powerful, emotion-laden memories at the time of investigation, not dispassionate clarity spanning three decades of a woman's interaction with her father and its effect on her. A daughter may say she hates her male parent, which is emotionally correct at the moment she utters it, but by no means is this the whole truth.

I am not implying that Freudian psychiatrists are all so naïve that they accept free association for truth. My point is that the technique can obscure balance and perspective by its emotional coloring. Increasing the duration of treatment from Freud's original three to six months to five years of analysis corrects these distortions to some extent.

TWO LIFE CYCLES:
FATHER'S AND DAUGHTER'S

The double-life-cycle approach is a new method to create order out of the thirty years of confusion, complexity, and emotional interaction between father and daughter. It is designed to help you integrate your thoughts and emotions and put them in perspective, so you can retain what you like and change what you want. It strives to compensate for two weaknesses in the Freudian approach: the excessive attention to early childhood and the strong influence of powerful emotions in the free-association process. This method is not designed to overlook feelings, but to sort them out and put them in perspective.

If a woman can recognize patterns and fully understand them she will be able to enjoy positive ones without guilt and change those she finds unacceptable. Control of the vastness of her relationship to her father is achieved by thinking about it in a disciplined way. Gone is childish egocentricity and her distorted view of him with its adverse effects on her subsequent life. She is able to experience her father holistically, to stand back and look at the complete mosaic and subtle fabric of her years with him. The double-life-cycle perspective enables her to see how they have loved, hated, hurt, and helped one another and what effect this continues to have on her life.

THE FATHER-DAUGHTER MODEL

This model divides the first thirty years of interaction between father and daughter into three parts, each of which is ten years long. It assumes the father is in his late twenties or early thirties when she is born and focuses on the main characteristics of each of them during the three decades. The first decade is called the *oasis* and occurs during her childhood and his thirties; the second is the *conflict*, during her adolescence and his forties; and the third is *separation*, during her twenties and his fifties. The pleasures and conflicts of each stage will be described below in brief detail. The model can be pictured as follows:

	AGE	
STAGE	DAUGHTER	FATHER
Oasis	Childhood	Thirties
Conflict	Adolescence	Forties
Separation	Adult	Fifties

Any model is by definition artificial. Its aim is to simplify and clarify, but it cannot fit every instance. Some fathers, for example, are over seventy when their daughters are born. A model does describe the most typical situations and helps delineate how those that do not fit differ. The father who is seventy or eighty when his daughter is in her teens is not in his own period of conflict when she is in hers. The model calls attention to this difference and helps a woman think about what effect it might have had on her development and subsequent relationships with men.

For the majority of daughters who do fit into the model it offers the following advantages. It orders the complexity of thirty years and encourages a woman to think systematically about them. How did you and your father interact when you were a child, an adolescent, in your twenties? It stimulates memory and fosters greater understanding of these periods in your life. Use of this model will minimize emotional distortions from any one of these decades and put them into the perspective of all three. Stormy adolescent reactions can be softened by memories of the oasis of childhood. As extreme feelings calm and take their place in the fabric of the full thirty years, a realistic view of the father will emerge, uncolored by worship or anger. This balanced comprehension of how your male parent has affected you will help you improve your present and future.

The Oasis

The first stage includes the girl's childhood and her father's thirties. The importance of the father in infant development is finally being discovered. The theoretical and research focus on the mother and infant had become excessive. The British psychiatrist John Bowlby, in his theory of attachment, described a unique bond between mother and infant that causes the baby to stay close to the protecting adult. Freud and Bowlby saw the mother-infant relationship as the foundation of all later love. The male parent's role was downplayed until recently when Milton Kotelchuck, a University of Massachusetts psychologist, and others found in six large, careful studies that infants cry and become upset when fathers leave them and are delighted and exhibit no stranger anxiety when they return. The nine-month-old baby's separation protest, a measure of its attachment, has been found to be the *same* for both parents. Margaret Mead has pointed out that forming attachments to more than one person has clear survival value, since the infant is thereby insured against loss of one of them. While infants become attached to both parents, there are some differences in style. As Michael E. Lamb explains in his excellent review *The Role of the Father in Child Development,*[*] play seems more prominent in fathers and caretaking in mothers.

Now that it seems well established that infants develop attachment behavior to both parents during the first nine months of life, the importance of the father-daughter relationship from the beginning is greater than previously suspected. Attachment is the preference for or desire to be close to a specific person, usually conceived of as stronger or wiser. Bowlby indicates that although it is especially evident during early childhood, this need is present from the cradle to the grave. He observed that these strong bonds arise without any reference to food. In 1958, the very same year he published his theory, Harlow found a young monkey would cling to a dummy that does not feed it provided it is soft and comfortable. Bowlby recorded emotional distress including anger, anxiety, and depression throughout life whenever the un-

---

[*] Michael E. Lamb, ed. (New York: John Wiley & Sons, Inc., 1976).

willing loss and separation from an attachment figure occurs. In early childhood it includes crying and calling to be cared for, clinging and following, and strong protest should a child be left alone or with strangers. In adults these feelings resurface most when the person is distressed, ill, or afraid.

Intense emotions arise during the formation, maintenance, and disruption of attachment relationships. Maintenance of the bond is experienced as a source of security.

Adult attachments are influenced by the experiences one has had with similar figures in childhood. There is a strong causal relationship between an individual's experiences with her parents and her later capacity to make affectional bonds. Past psychoanalytic theory describes girls discovering their fathers between the ages of three and six as a result of disappointment in their mothers and in themselves for not possessing a penis. Present knowledge shows father's influence to be earlier and even more significant, or in the words of the theory, not just oedipal but pre-oedipal.

The Oasis—Father

Typically father is in his third decade when his daughter is in her first. He is usually preoccupied with career building. Often this is at the expense of his marriage, his leisure, his friendships, his sex drive, and his time for introspection. He can be a relatively sexless working machine and in this sense he is in a kind of latency period akin to the latency of childhood which occurs between the ages of six and the onset of puberty. The latency period is one of emotional quiescence between the turmoil of childhood and adolescence. This period is the same as the fourth of Erik Erikson's Eight Stages of Man (Industry v. Inferiority) and is associated with the acquisition of skills. The father's thirties is a period during which he strives for the position he will achieve in his forties and fifties. While his child acquires skills he gains job status.

During this time in their lives his daughter may not see a lot of him, and this is one reason why the father's importance has been overlooked by researchers and theoreticians. What has only recently been noticed is that in many cases she sees *enough* of him to form an attachment in infancy. It is not certain what minimum number of hours or quality of interaction is necessary for this attachment to occur. Frequently it is assumed that because mother is there more hours it only occurs with her. But mothers may be in the same house with babies and spend very little time actually interacting with them. Several researchers have observed that even when mother is in the same room or carrying her child, social interaction may be minimal and infrequent. Furthermore, it is not the amount but the quality of time between parents and children that is most important. Daily separations from mothers in day-care centers do not hurt the infant-mother attachment. Daily separations from a working father are no more harmful.

The busyness of the "latent-period" father in his thirties, far from destroying his impact on his daughter's development, may heighten the quality of the time they spend together, since he allows himself few other pleasures and emotional outlets as he strives to get ahead and build his career. Michael Lamb and others have found in their research that the time spent by fathers and infants is very enjoyable and elicits highly positive emotions on both sides. It is this delight that has made me call this period an oasis for him from his cold, competitive world of striving for success. It is a time of pure pleasure and deep emotional attachment for him and as a consequence for her as well.

Of course this oasis is not always such a romantic, positive interlude. Often a tired man is called upon by his equally tired wife for child care, which is no longer a delight but a chore. An irritable, overworked father forced to change diapers is not a desirable attachment figure, at least for the moment. But nonetheless he loves his pretty little girl and usually the overall picture is positive.

The Oasis—Daughter

It is not very long before the baby to whom he has become attached becomes a little girl. According to Dr. John Money, sex roles are fixed by eighteen months. By this time she is walking, talking, in a dress, her hair styled, and she has a special smile for daddy. The second and third years of life are a period in which the child learns self-control, of which toilet training is one part. While the first-year parental task is the sensitive meeting of the infant's needs, the parents' role at the toddler stage is to set firm boundaries of acceptable behavior, while encouraging freedom, exploration, and self-sufficiency. The pattern of infancy continues into childhood, in which the mother is more involved in caretaking and the father in play. Discipline falls more to her, although both participate. In the fourth year play becomes a central activity for fun, mastery, the release of tension, and trying out adult roles. The fifth year is the culmination of childhood, a time when she is definitely his little girl and he her hero.

Father and daughter throughout the first six years of her life provide each other a happy respite from the rigors of daily life, he from the workaday world and she from mother's discipline and demands. This special holiday from care continues as one aspect of their attachment all their lives. He is tougher on his sons, as mother is on her daughters.

From age six to puberty, her latency period, he becomes more involved with her intellectual development and begins to be interested in her schoolwork and to teach her. Unfortunately, much research has focused on those fathers who have discouraged the growth of their daughter's minds and overlooked the many who are genuinely supportive.

THE LEGACY OF THE OASIS

The way a father treats his daughter in the oasis period makes an indelible impression on her. By overdoing it he may cause her to long all her life for this time when she was the center of his attention. As Proust, who was in awe of the power of the past, said, a human is a "creature without any fixed age, who has the faculty of becoming, in a few seconds, many years younger. . . ." For some women the delight of the oasis is etched for ever after and interferes with all adult love relationships. No man is as attentive and caring as her doting father.

If there was no happiness or too little, with her father in the oasis period a girl's femininity suffers. Their first decade together not only includes her need to form an infant's attachment but if the father is absent or angry and rejecting, leaves the girl completely discouraged in her beginning and most important efforts with a man. She has no experience of flirting with, gaining attention from, being worshiped by, or delighting the man who means the most to her at the most impressionable time in her life. Lamb cites four studies in the nineteen-sixties which all found that paternal masculinity was consistently associated with the femininity of daughters and inconsistently with the masculinity of sons. It is surprising that fathers affect their daughters' femininity more than their sons' masculinity. Researchers, theorists, and my own clinical and research experiences all concur that a good relationship with a warm and accepting father who is not too frightened of her sexuality is extremely important to a little girl. Someone who can enjoy her beauty, her smile, her pretty dress, her first efforts at makeup and jewelry, helps her gain the confidence that she can attract, charm, and interest a man. A father who is made nervous by and ridicules her little feminine gestures, or who is always too tired or angry to be pleased by them, or who is absent too much, can cause his daughter to be insecure about her body and her ability to attract a man. Fortunately, older brothers, uncles, or other males present on a continuing basis can undo some of the damage caused by the absent, withdrawn, or rejecting father.

Too little or no childhood closeness to an accepting father can leave a woman with various kinds of scars; insecurity is one of the deepest. Detachment is another because she does not know how to be close to a man and feels cut off. Not frightened necessarily, she simply does not expect love, closeness, warmth, or intimacy from a male. Anger is another unhappy legacy from this period. If the most important man in her life, her father, has not given her the love and attention she needed, a woman is left deeply enraged. As soon as her husband or lover makes a slip or lets her down in even the smallest way her fury bursts forth. Her rageful, righteous indignation at his social slip, drinking, crudeness, wandering eye, dullness, is too great, fueled by her anger at her father's neglect. Her hostility drives men away, while punishing any who remain.

Some women, deprived in their childhood of father's warmth, may be sexless as adults. Sexless does not necessarily mean spinsterish, virginal, or even anorgasmic, although it can exhibit itself in these ways. Rather it means the absence of desire for men. A girl who has not been aroused by her father's attention is unlikely to feel strong sexual passions as a woman. She grows into a wife who can perform sexually for her husband but has no interest in him or anyone else. Adult sexual fantasies and desires have their basis in childhood experiences and longings. Modified through the years, they represent a woman's lifelong story and her father played a key role in what excites her years later.

The absent or rejecting father can also leave a woman with excessive hunger for male attention, very demanding that her lover be totally devoted and quick to anger and throw her partner out should he fail her. Another manifestation of father deprivation is addiction to the excitement of the courtship and intolerance of the calmness of the long term. These women crave the daily flowers and phone calls, lust for the new man, but become bored and depressed once the affair calms down. Unreasonably quick to feel ignored and hurt, as the veneer of excitement wears off, their childhood pain resurfaces and they rush off to the narcotic of a new love.

If the poisoned or absent oasis is harmful, then equally dangerous is the overbearing one. Fathers who are too needful of the worship of their little girls, who are too disappointed in the real world and revel in this escape, cling too long, and try to stunt the growth and independence of their developing children, can bring up women who never leave psychologically. Some, when interviewed, are quite open about saying how none of their men measure up to their fathers, who are brighter, more considerate, and better company.

Some women are unaware of their continuing childlike escape from responsibility and of how their lovers' requests seem excessive next to their fathers' giving. It is hard for them to realize they anticipate too much, since they have had no experience with a gradual increase in responsibility as they were growing up. After they've been babied all their lives by their fathers, husbands and lovers seem harsh and excessively demanding. Such women may never leave their fathers at all or if they marry are unable to be happy with another man.

The effect of the disturbed oasis is not everlasting. Women can get over it if they do two things: recognize what their fathers were like and how it currently affects them and try to change their pattern. The damage from early childhood can be undone. Human beings are very flexible. They can adapt new ways once they know they must. Childhood unhappinesses are harder to overcome than those from adolescence or the twenties. Knowledge of the self, determination to change, and the courage to try different behavior is what is required.

CONFLICT: HIS FORTIES, HER TEENS

The period of midlife has been compared to adolescence. For both father and daughter it is a time of separation as she leaves the oasis they shared. For each it is a time of questioning. She asks "Who am I?" He wonders who he will continue to be. She rebels against authority and convention, he wonders if he can stand one more board meeting or dinner party. Both may be moody. Each may be concerned with the great existential questions of life and death, the brevity of time, and the physical changes of age. Both may be restless and discontented.

Father in his forties is reevaluating his existence and wondering if he will continue his career and private life as it is in the time left to him, which he now sees as limited. Would it be wise for him to change jobs or careers? Does he still love his wife? Does he have friends and does he see them enough? Is he using his talents and being creative? Does he enjoy his life or has it become an empty shell?

But the father does not have the leisure to reflect that his adolescent daughter does. There are great financial pressures in meeting the high costs of education and supporting the family. Concerned about the young men coming up the ladder behind him, he may fear losing his job or failing to get an important promotion. He worries about his health and aging. And he watches his little girl grow to womanhood and prepare to leave him.

The adolescent daughter sees her father differently because she is no longer a little, worshipful girl and also because he in fact has changed. Typically, in his thirties he worked constantly to build his career and resembled an emotionally quiescent latency child. Now in his forties he is more like an adolescent himself, more sexual, harder-drinking, moodier, and likelier to get into trouble with work or women. But this is not necessarily bad for her. Fathers who do not develop and change over the decades can give daughters an unrealistic idea of what men are. Men who hide their faults or continue their thirties latency into the forties and fifties linger on as oasis heroes to their daughters. Such women remain children in their relations to men, expecting lovers also to be pure heroes, endlessly patient and supportive, encouraging and forgiving, never demanding—in short, fathers to little girls.

Although adolescent girls become upset as they discover the flaws in their fathers, it is a disturbance that is ultimately

good for them. The daughter can become very angry and attack her father for his irresponsibility, his drinking, womanizing, gambling, or spendthrift behaviors, as well as for the
deficits in his character, his rigidity, conservatism, fearfulness,
or lack of business success.

There are, therefore, two factors operating to help the adolescent gain a more realistic view of her father. First, simply
being older enables her to see the real weaknesses that he like
all humans possesses; and second, he may in fact behave
badly. The two combine to ensure his *fall from grace*. Now if
the fall is too far or too abrupt it can cause lasting effects.
The father who deserts his family suddenly and never sees
them again can leave a daughter forever afraid to allow herself to be vulnerable to a man, sure that he too will leave her.
But if the fall from grace is not too severe and if he accepts
the anger and criticism arising from her disappointment in
him, then two good things will happen. It will help her to
separate from him and it will encourage her to have reasonable adult expectations of her lovers, rather than unrealistic
and childish ones.

Most fathers struggle to maintain their hero image with
their daughters and become too upset about revealing their
human weaknesses. This reluctance is akin to the daughter's
wish to remain a pure virgin in his eyes. Each wants to hold
on to the happy childhood days and not face the realities of
life. Partly it is a vestige from the puritan past. Fathers and
daughters are supposed to be pure, noble, selfless, cheerful,
and never angry. This ideal causes them to try to keep up
pretenses and present an unrealistic image to each other.
When fathers fail—and many more do than want to—in their
careers, by becoming ill and weak, by drinking too much, or
by committing adultery, they feel excessively guilty and upset

with themselves and unable to accept the attack of the disappointed daughter. Many women describe fathers who speak superficially to them and never express feelings. Often it is not just the parent but the daughter as well who cannot face the reality of adult sexuality. They are both unable to voice their anger and disappointment that neither lived up to the fiction of the oasis. Both have faults which they find hard to face in themselves and each other.

Even a father who admits his own shortcomings and is not a guilty person will find it hard to deal with his adolescent daughter. In the early half of her teens she is uncomfortable about her body, may be moody and short-tempered, and becomes filled with embarrassment at the smallest thing he does. Even though he wants to hold on to her he must let her go. She will have to face dangers and challenges without him. He must help her to grow independent of him, to be self-sufficient and able to find her own way without his direction.

She wants autonomy but still needs his aid. She perceives his help as interference, advice as orders, and concern as babying. He must find a way to help her even though it is resented, offer advice that she won't follow, and talk to her although his attention is taken for an attack. Fathers who are too preoccupied with their own midlife problems are usually short on patience and willingness to take the time to negotiate delicately with their touchy teenage daughters. As a result they issue angry orders and engage in stormy battles with their girls or else they just withdraw and become absent.

Angry, tired fathers seem more available to daughters for fighting than for joy. Rebellion is flamed as a contest of wills ensues over rules, growing independence, excessive concern about safety, and, too often, ultimately over whether to let her grow and go or keep her with him. She struggles to get away but also wants to continue to please him so he will still love and care. She strives to be noticed if he is absent too much, to be private if he pries into her private life too intrusively, to be respected if he is intolerant of her adolescent sloppiness.

Their second decade together can leave lifelong scars which harm her relationships with men by repeating the anger, rebellion, and excessive fighting. Unable to be a fully functioning, separate woman when involved in a love affair, she longs for the childhood oasis. If a father takes pleasure in his adolescent daughter, talks to her about philosophical, poetic, or aesthetic matters, or current events, then sharing the growth, ideas, sensitivities, and intelligence of her youth can bring joy to both. Good memories of long talks and beautiful walks from this era allow a woman to enjoy her lover's mind, to be close to him philosophically, romantically, and sexually, and to forgive his faults and permit him to be human.

SEPARATION

The process of separation, of becoming a self-sufficient person, begins in infancy. Especially during the first three years but throughout childhood and adolescence, the capacity is established to stand on one's own. Parents have powerful influence on whether their children become strong and able to leave them as adults. Fathers can cling to their daughters at every stage or they can encourage them out of the nest.

When a woman reaches her twenties if she has successfully grown through her childhood and adolescence she is ready to physically and emotionally leave her family. The geographical step is much easier taken than the psychological. In every adult there is within a helpless child afraid of being alone. Separation, therefore, causes everyone anxiety.

The question is, what is she leaving? Is it someone who is necessary for her survival or parents who have helped her be able to confidently care for herself? No daughter leaves home without fear, ambivalence, and mourning. The process takes varying amounts of time depending upon the strength of the woman, her psychological maturity, and the support of her parents.

In the process of separation the daughter *detaches* her feelings from her father. This is accomplished by moving physically and emotionally away from him. As they come in contact less frequently the strength of their psychological attachment subsides. This is aided by her increasing involvement with others in her intimate life and in her work. The process is not always smooth and gradual. Sometimes father and daughter fight as they break apart and they may speak to each other rarely if at all. Their parting of company is accompanied by distress and sadness on each side. When the pain becomes too great they may totally withdraw, fight, or slip back to a closer, childlike way for a time. But once the emotional time is over, the daughter is able to take her feelings from her father and be able to reinvest them in others. She is then free to find a man and a life of her own.

During her twenties a woman modifies her needs and emotions. The swings of mood, characteristic of the adolescent, become less extreme. She evolves from the *af*fective (emotional) state of the adolescent to the *ef*fective (masterful) status of the adult. She is less inclined to get upset about events and more willing to do something about them.

In this process, during which she becomes the master of her feelings rather than their slave, her anger matures. From the temper tantrum of the two-year-old who cannot stand frustration and believes herself entitled to what she wants to the argumentative adolescent who engages in critical battles with the restricting parent she becomes able to feel the appropriate angry response of the adult. Neither excessively meek because of fear she will completely lose control and explode in rage nor quick to flare in impulsive adolescent anger, she is able to feel her wrath, control it, and express it at the appropriate time when it is in her own interest.

The resolution within the woman in her twenties of her feelings about the Fall of Father helps her gain control of herself, feel strong, and be able to separate. She has behind her in adolescence the feeling of anger and disappointment toward him which helped her begin to leave him. The process of reconciliation between them releases her feelings. If she continues her adolescent anger toward him throughout her twenties her emotions (in spite of being negative) will continue to be tied up with him. By forgiving him and accepting him with his faults she finds it much easier to leave.

The Father and Separation

Father is in his fifties as his daughter is leaving. If his career and marriage are going well he is of course able to tolerate it much better. But nonetheless he is saddened and goes into a state of mourning. Psychologically well put together men accept the pain, suffer it, get over it, and go on with a new phase of their lives. More unstable ones attempt to hold on to their daughters or may create emotional scenes of anger and despair. If a woman is lucky her father will help her leave, push her forcibly out the door if necessary. He will calm her fears and encourage her to go out and live her independent life, while remaining available to her should she need him. He will accept her as another adult, not as a little girl. All this adjusting takes time and rarely proceeds smoothly. Emotions are strong and few men are perfect. There may be tears, anger, and attempts to cling. It takes fathers years to adjust to the adult status of their daughters.

The Daughter and Separation

A young woman in her twenties knows her parents are no longer necessary for her survival, yet she is not always quite certain. She feels anxious about going out on her own and dreads leaving the father who is capable of protecting her and relieving her fears. Her attempt to go may be counteracted by anxiety which completely paralyzes her. She may pick a fight with her father and depart in a rage.

Once physically away from her father she must work on her part of the emotional separation from him. If she relies on him too much, turns to him with every problem, the necessary work of mourning and detaching her feelings from him will be interfered with. Some young women go to the opposite extreme and have nothing to do with their fathers. In assuming that any turning to their fathers is a total surrender they tightly close off their dependent wishes without working on them. Thus they avoid experiencing the sadness of losing their fathers, but they also subvert the emotional process of separation. They are unable to freely interact with their fathers as equal adults and their feelings are not truly freed up for others.

The young woman who tolerates the pain of separation from her father and recognizes his loss becomes a true adult who wants to see her father and is not afraid of being overwhelmed by his care or her desire for it. No longer afraid of being a dependent child in his presence, she is able to share her life generously with him. This is a source of continuing pleasure to both of them.

STYLES OF INDEPENDENCE

According to Jung, individuation is the realization that one is separate and different from others and that one is a whole and indivisible person. Individuation is completed in middle age. The process of maturation does not end at age thirty.

Otto Rank believed men and women go through three stages in the process of individuation. In the first the individual wills for herself that which her parents and society have decided for her and her ideal is to be like others. Rank considered the average person to be fixed at this stage. In the second there is conflict with the community, whose standards she cannot accept, but she remains unable to construct her own principles. The final stage reveals a truly autonomous individual with creative use of her own powers and ideas. She is not driven by Freudian instincts and prohibitions, but is responsible, conscious, ethical, and creative.

THEORIES OF PERSONALITY DEVELOPMENT

Freud thought that the child developed by learning to restrain and inhibit his or her instincts when confronted by the outside world. But from the very beginning his Viennese colleague Alfred Adler emphasized the importance of the social milieu along with the individual's goal of overcoming infantile inferiority and striving toward superiority and challenged the Freudian concept of biologically determined psychosexual stages of development.

As European psychoanalysts such as Erich Fromm, Franz Alexander, and Karen Horney came to America, they found Freud's theories less applicable. They believed the influence of culture was more important than that of sexual instinct.

The impact of the Oedipus complex, for example, was thought to be determined by the power structure of the family and the subtle seductiveness of the parents, rather than to be inherited and biologically innate as Freud believed. Harry Stack Sullivan, now generally recognized as the most important American-born psychiatrist, thought it more scientific and productive to take a skeptical, scientific view of this important Freudian concept. Rather than assume everyone had an Oedipus complex, a theory based on evidence from a few intensively psychoanalyzed patients, he investigated with an open mind and found some individuals who did not seem to have this "universal" sexual desire for the parent of the opposite sex.

Another example of a Freudian concept based on little evidence is that of penis envy. To be brief, since this notion has been broadly attacked and is largely out of favor, it is another example of how Freud did not realize the effect of his own time and place on his theory. He believed the female experiences the lack of a penis as a loss and envies the male. It is penis envy, he thought, that makes women competitive and aggressive. This thought originated from his turn-of-the-century Viennese notion of the primacy of the male. The American Sullivan, studying women without preconceived notions, attributed their competitive and aggressive strivings to natural wishes for achievement and a desire to overcome cultural restrictions.

Sullivan believed that humans, in addition to their biological requirements, also have need for status, recognition, and a relationship with others. Self-esteem comes from the capacity to deal effectively with the anxiety an individual experiences in her daily life. Anxiety is caused by receiving disapproval from a significant adult and is alleviated by gaining approval. Sullivan's theory stressed the interpersonal while Freud's focused on the internal biological. Sullivan's is more capable of objective verification. The withdrawal of approval, for example, can be observed, while an unconscious impulse cannot.

KINDS OF AMERICAN WOMEN

Anxiety and confusion are rampant in America for both sexes. Our society is evolving and changing so fast that women do not know whether to be virgins, promiscuous, sex objects, brains, mothers, housewives, workaholics, married, divorced, single, faithful, or adulterers, or to try to do it all at once in a high-powered seventy-hour career combined with attentive motherhood and warm wifeliness. There is no specific mode of behavior expected for which there is support by a completely accepted psychological theory. As a result, it is very unclear how a father should bring his daughter up or how he should relate to her once she is an adult. Experts give parents much the same instructions training analysts do student psychoanalysts: Be there! Be accepting! Don't judge excessively! But although this is good advice and will help fathers and daughters stay out of fights, it all seems pretty bloodless and cold. Should a father tell a fully grown daughter what she needs to but does not want to hear at the risk of making her mad and should she do the same? Should their adult relationship be distant and clinical or can it continue emotional and intimate? What is normal? Any psychoanalyst with proper credentials and a definite recipe for how to behave is followed hungrily, because modern fathers and daughters do not know how to act either separately or with one another.

Should daughters be brought up to live close? What if they marry a corporate man who has to move a dozen times as his career advances? How will such a woman do with him? Or should she be brought up ready to move and travel? Does this mean preparing for separation and independence too early with the resulting cold and distant family which never truly enjoys one another?

How much should a father and daughter separate in her twenties? Should a woman be prepared to stand on her own two feet, to adjust to a modern, lonely reality, or, alternatively, should she be held in the warmth and support of the extended family with its emotional economic interdependence? The upbringing for modern corporate life, for frequent moves and adjustments, is not the same as that for the woman who will live her whole life around the corner from her family. Yet both are normal and American.

There are several ways to look at normality. One view is health, the absence of psychopathology. A second encompasses the ideal, the optimal in functioning. A third is average, what most people are like. What is psychologically normal for modern American daughters is not one ideal average. We are a pluralistic society composed of many different healthy ways to behave.

There are, really, no universal rules regarding how fathers and adult daughters should treat each other. But if their relationship prevents her from finding a man of her own, if it unduly influences her in the kind of man she finds or makes her relate badly to him, then something is wrong.

SELF-AWARENESS

We all carry vestiges of youth which leave parts of us psychologically undeveloped. Even the most grown-up person retains elements of childhood and adolescent emotional and behavioral patterns. Since we like to think of ourselves as responsible we find our continuing immaturities embarrassing and difficult to face.

For a woman to understand herself she must be fully aware of the child, adolescent, and adult facets of her personality. She has to know when her immaturities are most likely to cloud her reasoning and to guard against their excessive sway. No one is able to eliminate all of the irrational within her. Even if possible it would be unfortunate since emotions color our lives and make them more exciting and worthwhile.

Childlike and adolescent attributes are more likely to trouble us at home with our intimates than out in the world. (Sometimes the reverse is true and an oasis girl is comfortable with her autocratic husband, but cannot cope with a promotion at work.) Our youthful traces show in different parts of our lives at various times. Understanding how and why a particular circumstance threatens rationality makes us more able to cope with it effectively.

For a woman to comprehend herself and overcome her difficulties she must know what it is in her that perpetuates them and under what circumstances they arise. Her problems may occur mainly with her long-term relationships, be primarily sexual or restricted to her career, or affect her overall self-esteem.

Because it is so hard to truly see oneself clearly and dispassionately, a main aim of this book is to help women do so in a systematic and effective way. Early experiences with parents powerfully influence the shaping of personality and character. These then become so automatic a part of a person they are hard to view objectively. Most psychiatric and psychological theories of the twentieth century have focused on mothers as the prime shapers of a youth's psyche. More recent researchers have begun to give father his due. This new emphasis is motivated partly by the male's increased role in child rearing as his wife works full time. But even during previous times of lesser participation the paternal role has been wrongfully and excessively ignored. Even fathers described as busy, always working, passive, and withdrawn have profound effects on their daughters. For a woman to glibly dismiss her father as a nice man always away at his office, on his sailboat, or out with his friends is to ignore the opportunity to understand him, herself, their interaction and his full effect on her life with lovers, at work, in sex, on her personality and behavior. She who has not studied her own history is destined to repeat its mistakes, to thoughtlessly act like her father when she does not want to or to rebel against his ways even when to do so harms her.

Many interviews, scores of them over prolonged periods, reveal that most women do not and cannot see their fathers accurately, and are unaware of the many ways they have shaped and continue to affect their lives long after they have left home. Thinking about their first thirty years in stages helps a woman clarify her father's continuing influence. Only then does the gradual, changing, subtle effect begin to stand out in sharp relief. Previously unnoticed paternal influences on the mind and actions become obvious. Only by the wisdom gained through calmly reviewing the touching of their two life cycles over thirty years will she be able to free herself of his hold.

Two

SEX

It is not surprising that a woman's sexuality is powerfully influenced by her relationship to her father. Because it occurs steadily over thirty years, the effect can be almost imperceptible or at least largely unnoticed. A woman may never fully understand how her sexual style has been colored by her father because it is so much a part of her that it is difficult to see. Sexual reactions happen quickly and automatically. Women like dark- or light-haired men, intellectuals or athletes, talkers or the silent—in a flash, chemically. Only upon reflection, after the heat of attraction and excitement has cooled, do recognizable patterns emerge. The few women for whom sex has gone smoothly with their first and only lover need never reflect on the cause of their attraction. Such women can remain unaware and content. For the overwhelming majority of persons who have sexual problems, however, there is an advantage in understanding the origins of their attractions. For any woman, one very dominating influence is her father. He is the first man to whom she gives her heart and how he reacts strongly affects her future with men.

The influence of the father does not crystallize in some Oedipal drama at age four; it is a process that goes on for thirty years. The sexual styles of father and daughter reinforce each other over three decades. If she bats her eyelashes, he can smile and respond, stimulating her coquettishness. Conversely, he might frown and thus encourage her to be more reserved. If your father liked women and delighted in their sensuality, then he rewarded that side of you. If he found feminine wiles threatening, your ability to flirt and engage in courtship play may be deeply buried. Between the sensual and the abstinent are many gradations. The level at which your style is set largely depends upon how warmly your father behaved toward you, though it is so ingrained you probably hardly notice.

Sexual fantasy is poorly understood in psychiatry. We know nearly everyone has erotic fantasies, but why they take the form they do and how they change over the years has been inadequately investigated. In the excellent book *Sexual Excitement* (New York: Pantheon Books, 1979), West Coast psychoanalyst Robert Stoller comments that sexual fantasy is an exciting story people continuously write in their minds, modifying it as their experiences change and grow. It is like a fairy tale or personal myth filled with deep psychological meanings. Father has a profound influence on your mind and what excites it sexually. He is in your lusty dreams, although in disguise, and in your daytime erotic reveries. When the stranger at a party fills you with desire, your father's influence contributes to the attraction. What you consider handsome or arousing has been subtly shaped by him and you together. Sexual fantasy is not all sweetness and romance. Dr. Stoller points out in his study that much of it is composed of aggression, hostility, and a desire to conquer. His sample, however, was composed of psychoanalytic patients and his findings, therefore, are biased. My own study, which dealt with a large non-psychiatric group, shows a greater diversity of theme in erotic fantasy. The unknown, the exotic, the unattainable, the helpless, the powerful—all figure in the fantasy life of women. The themes of sexual excitement were found to be quite various, but what they had in common was the prominence of the father, often unrecognized by the subject.

The dynamic interplay in real life of the two developing and changing persons—father and daughter—shape these fantasies. In her first thirty years, a daughter passes through many roles. She is the little girl pushing her carriage, then the awkward pubescent, the defiant adolescent, the college student (away from home), the graduate, the career woman. All of these changes in her affect a father. Nor is his life static. In his thirties he concentrates on his career, in his forties he takes stock, and then he calms down in his fifties. The changes in each of their lives influence the content of a daughter's desires.

No two dynamically changing persons can remain in perfect harmony over three decades. A father is good with and for his daughter at certain ages and in specific ways. One coaches his daughter beautifully in mathematics, but does not want to hear about how she gets on with her friends at school. Another glows when his three-year-old imitates her mother but shows no interest when she is fully grown. Was your father frightened of your firm, adolescent body or was he overly interested? Did he make bad jokes, adding to your awkwardness, or parade around nude in front of you, thus embarrassing or overstimulating you? Was your father delighted by the questioning and sensitivity of your adolescence or harsh and punitive toward what he considered the frivolity of your philosophical and poetic inquiries?

Behavior which is rewarded persists and is repeated while that which is ignored or punished is given up because it does not produce results. The child seeks attention from the parent and employs behavior that works and is reinforced. If a father responds to the sexuality of his daughter in all its different forms as she grows, this side of her will be prominent. If he is threatened, uninterested, or absent, her sexuality might be harmed. It is usual to be hurt during childhood by parental imperfections and deficiencies, but human beings are resilient. It takes determination to change oneself and overcome the scars of childhood, but almost all of the sexual ill effects of imperfect fathers on daughters can be undone. First, however, they must be recognized.

Because it is the rare father who is perfectly adept at dealing with all phases of his daughter's developing sexuality, almost every woman grows up impaired by her father's faults and mistaken reactions. There are few problem-free women. The prerequisites for healthy sexual attitudes and behavior are many and complex. A woman must acquaint herself with the intricacies of her body, overcome childhood inhibitions, learn to communicate her self-knowledge to a partner in an unthreatening way, and, finally, find a suitable man with whom to share sustained intimacy. None of these accomplishments is easy or simple.

No wonder Kinsey found that women do not reach their sexual peak until their thirties. Although the average female now loses her virginity in her late teens or early twenties, it takes her ten or more years until she is able to enjoy and participate fully in sexual intimacy. She must not only know herself and relax with her partner, but she must also understand, integrate, and break away from her father's influence. Kinsey's finding provided one key reason for my decision to consider the first thirty years of father-daughter interaction rather than just the first twenty. Although age eighteen or twenty-one defines legal adulthood, a woman does not reach sexual maturity until her thirties. One important reason for the delay is the continuing psychological attachment to the father, an attachment that prevents attainment of full erotic satisfaction.

PHYSICAL VIRGINITY AND PSYCHOLOGICAL VIRGINITY

After scores of interviews with women it has become clear to me that there are two kinds of virginity: physical and psychological. The first is lost in an often nervous act committed in the late teens or early twenties; the latter is forfeited when a woman, having freed herself of her father's hold, is able to give herself fully to her man. The loss of psychological virginity involves a process of thirty years, beginning in early childhood and ending with the achievement of open and gratifying sexual relations with a man on an intimate and continuing basis. This sexual evolution entails a separation from the father, to whom the daughter has been physically and emotionally tied.

If you and your father were too close or too distant you should expect some difficulty in achieving the maturity necessary to lose your psychological virginity. If you and he were sufficiently intimate to allow you to practice being a woman and yet distant enough to allow you your freedom, the task will be easier. The strength of the psychological and sexual tie between the two of you strongly affects your capacity to relate to men. Women attached to their fathers are not truly available to their husbands or lovers, while those who have never known their fathers emotionally and sexually are underdeveloped in relating to other men.

One thirty-year-old woman I interviewed was very close to her father intellectually. She learned so much from him that she went into a business similar to his and became very successful. Yet their relationship, so strong and sympathetic mentally, was not expressed physically. When, as a little girl, she craved a loving response from him, she received cold rationality instead. As a result she had male colleagues who admired her but she had no lovers. She had no idea how to attract a man. The only way she could be close to a man was in a businesslike way. Her body had not learned to speak.

To know your father sexually does not mean to know him incestuously. It means that you experience him as a man and that he responds to your femininity, first when you are a girl and then when you are a woman. How your eyes meet, whether or not you touch, the ways you play together, become the prototype from which you will later develop a style with your lovers.

While some women are actively aware of the influence of their fathers on their sexual problems, a much larger number are not. Some realize, for instance, the effect of a father complex and can see it operate in other women, but they remain completely blind to their own difficulties. It is common for a woman to overlook the subtle disruption of her love life by the effect of thirty years' interaction with her father. If she could see herself and her life more clearly, she would more likely solve her problems.

There is often a huge discrepancy between what a woman thinks is the cause of her difficulties and what actually is. One woman, for example, rapidly became bored by her lovers. She thought of herself as restless and dissatisfied. Four years of therapy had not improved her ability to sustain intimacy. She had come to recognize many facts about her father but the information had not been helpful in solving her dilemma.

She admitted that she had always been and remained her father's favorite child, being better-looking and brighter than her siblings. She also displaced her mother in her father's affections. Her mother was a depressed and dissatisfied woman who demanded her husband's attention and offered little or no pleasure in return. It was the daughter who delighted him. He took her shopping for clothes and discussed his business problems with her. She offered him bright and sound suggestions. They enjoyed each other's company immensely and she acknowledged their mutual admiration.

She also described clearly and lamented her difficulty in finding satisfaction in a long-term relationship with a lover. What she could not see was how the intimacy with her father impaired her ability to find intimacy with another man. She did not realize how attached she was to her interesting and charming father, nor how good she felt in his company and how bereft she felt without him.

With guidance, she scrutinized the quality of her emotions when she was with her father. She then examined the pattern of her love affairs—an invariable shift from initial excitement to ennui within months. She finally saw that her relationship with her father made any other involvements pale by comparison. Yet the critical realization did not signal an immediate shift away from him. She still found it difficult to substitute the long-term, sometimes dull reality with a man of her own for the excitement of being her father's first and continuing love. Unfortunately, the recognition of how one is spoiled does not always make one want to stop being so. No one relinquishes a pleasure unless either forced to or in the immediate hope of gaining a greater one. The hope of achieving the real satisfactions of a mature relationship with a man other than her father was not yet sufficiently strong to compel her to relinquish the fantasy association of childhood and adolescence.

In this case, the father had possessed his daughter for thirty-two years and the two of them would not let go of each other easily. The example is not offered as a dispiriting note, but to emphasize the difficulty women can have seeing problems with lovers and discussing how problems have roots in the past. It can be hard to give up the role of the little girl, especially when it has been and continues to be too gratifying.

LOSS OF PHYSICAL VIRGINITY

The hymen guards the door to womanhood, and so long as it remains shut the little girl is safe, protected and valued by her father whose place has not yet been taken by another man. Fathers and daughters seldom speak directly about virginity, yet however unspoken the issue, it is one of intense emotion. Without saying or perhaps even realizing why, he will insist she be home by a certain time—often much too early—and become irrationally angry if she disobeys. He seems convinced she will remain chaste if she is home before midnight, and equally certain that she will lose her virginity if she stays out until 1 A.M. While one father may hit his daughter and call her a tramp if she defies him and stays out too late, another may engage in an anxious and angry scene without the appropriate words.

Why are fathers and daughters so tense about chastity? Because loss of virginity is a secret, threatening rite of passage, unlike other rites which are held in the open and given parental support. No one protests the onset of menstruation. It is an involuntary, naturally occurring phenomenon that the family accepts. Other milestones are also welcomed and supported: first communions, bas mitzvahs, confirmations, graduations, and coming-out parties. Loss of virginity, on the other hand, usually happens in secret with conflicted feelings experienced by all involved: the young woman, her father and family, and even her lover. The good little girl passes nervously through her first complete erotic experience. Unsupported by her family, often condemned by herself, she fears she will lose her father and even the young man to whom she has hesitantly entrusted herself. For a young woman, the first sexual relationship is usually frightening. Because of her father's opposition and her own fears about losing his love and their mutual oasis, it generally takes ten or more years for women to feel relaxed and sexually secure.

Let us assume sexual intercourse occurs for the first time at age twenty. The young woman who engages in this act has a history of twenty years with her father, a period in which he has either responded to or rejected her femininity. Aspects of that history, such as the age at which she most pleased him or the features which he favored, become factors in her approach to and attitude toward her first full love affair.

When a woman waits until her late teens or early twenties to lose her virginity, it indicates that whatever relationship she has had with her father has been adequate to allow her to grow up before becoming physically intimate with a man of her own. Most often, girls who have intercourse in their early or mid-teens (ages thirteen to seventeen) have been raised in homes in which their experiences with their fathers have been troubled. The failure of fathers to attend to their early teenage daughters can result in a desperate search for male substitutes. Premature sexual intercourse is the product of the quest.

The woman who loses her virginity in her late teens or early twenties still jeopardizes her relationship with her father. Her mature sexuality threatens her position as "daddy's little girl," a position secured in a period in which her father exempted her from responsibility and judgment and provided her with a world of delight and love, without sex or fighting. With a sexless, romantic, almost religious love, father and daughter worshiped each other. This memory of childhood, comfortable and delicious, is precious to them both; neither wants to surrender it.

If a woman's father is overly binding, her initial physical intimacy may be an impulsive, drunken, guilt-ridden effort to break the hold he has on her. The daughter wants to escape the paternal grip and free herself from her own desire to hold on to their happy times together. One nervous nineteen-year-old college student let a male classmate convince her to go to bed with him. Within two weeks, her lover was avoiding her. When confronted, he said he wanted to date others because he was not yet ready to be involved with one woman. Her disappointment was overwhelming. She became very depressed as she began to learn the hard lesson that she could not remain "daddy's little girl" by transferring her dependency to a young man who would assume a parental role. She slept with six more young men in an effort to find one who would take care of her, but she was repeatedly disappointed. She became increasingly wild and uncontrolled, having sex with strangers, many of them unsavory characters. Her father tried to take care of her in the old way but she rebuffed his efforts. She found a man her father's age and the relationship worked for a while, but it also ended unhappily.

An inattentive father, on the other hand, robs his daughter of experience and skills which would enhance her first full love affair. A father who is unsettled or frightened by his adolescent daughter's body and sexuality may retreat into work or behind the newspaper, leaving parental conversation and advice to the mother. Unaccustomed to talking to or arguing with her male parent, the daughter never acquires the savvy needed to size up a man. She is handicapped in selecting a husband or lover wisely and ill equipped to negotiate problems which arise in love.

Sexual intercourse requires subtle and delicate communication between partners. A daughter learns the subtleties of dialogue from her father and practices them with him. She usually charms and delights her father in the oasis years, but as an adolescent she discusses reality, negotiates differences, bumps into the limits he sets, and encounters his resulting anger. A woman who has not had the experience of negotiating with her father during her teen years, and consequently has not learned to control her feelings when denied her own way, has difficulty coping with the intense feelings arising from sexual intimacy. Since it is the rare father and daughter who get on well consistently throughout her adolescence, it is no wonder that most women do not sail smoothly through their first love affair. Fathers and daughters require a third decade (her twenties) to help her mature and separate fully. Since almost no woman waits until she is psychologically mature and in her thirties to lose her virginity, she usually has trouble with her first and indeed first few love affairs. Of course, her early lovers are also immature, which contributes to the problems.

Should a woman wait until she is thirty to have intercourse, thus ensuring simultaneous physical and psychological loss of virginity? This question is largely theoretical since very few wait until age thirty and those who do are usually inhibited and troubled in another way. Not all are, however. Even now, a small percentage of women wait for sex until marriage. Some in that group marry quite late—in their late twenties or early thirties. In my experience such women do no better than those who have lost their physical virginity between ages seventeen and twenty-two. In fact, they have some catching up to do.

It is the fortunate adolescent girl who has a warm, not seductive, and attentive, not interfering, father who brings reasonable patience to bear upon her rebellion and aggression. When she is fourteen or fifteen she can shout at him "I hate you" and he will not retaliate too angrily or withdraw from her. They both try as well as they can to adjust to her becoming a sexual woman, rather than pretending she is still a little girl. He enjoys seeing her body mature without comment or fear. As he accepts her sexual development, so will she, although both are a little uncomfortable about it. Paternal responsiveness and acceptance help a woman to grow sexually. By trying not to rival her boyfriends, not to be brighter and more attractive than they, but to act the part of father even when it requires stands which are unpopular with her and make her angry, he allows someone to take her away from him.

If through adolescence you stayed a little girl basking in the soft, warm, uncritical glow of your father, you can be deflowered in the physical sense while remaining "intact" psychologically. For every woman, the first sexual encounter is both a nervous experiment and a step away from father and, for these reasons, deeply disturbing. It is not surprising that some women take years to achieve satisfactory sexual relations.

THE NERVOUS FIRST TIME

Every woman remembers losing her virginity and points to that time as a starting point for thinking about her sexual life. Any nervously made decision usually reveals signs of anxiety upon examination. For example, first intercourse usually takes place spontaneously or impulsively, without planning or assumption of appropriate responsibility. It is too difficult for a virginal daughter to acknowledge and accept openly such responsibility.

Nervous decisions often evolve from passive, confused feelings; they are not the outcome of measured choice. The loss of physical virginity is a big step from which there is no going back. Though a woman should be able to think through to a clear decision whether or not to have sex for the first time, the idea of defloration can be so threatening to some women that the actual event has to be experienced passively as though they were out of control and overwhelmed by desire. A woman may see the man as having forced her through insistence or pleas of need. Thus, she must take the difficult step under feelings of coercion, desire, or intoxication. It is hard for a woman to feel she has made pure, active rational choices about losing her virginity when torn by the fear of losing her father's love. Actively opposed or unsupported steps into adulthood are hard to make.

Most young women interviewed were primarily concerned about their fathers' reaction to their loss of virginity. Some feared his wrath; others, his pain. Things would never be the same between them again. The cushion of the oasis gone, they feared losing their fathers' love and acceptance. Some took the step because they didn't want to lose their lovers as well, lovers who threatened to leave them if they refused to have intercourse. What should be a free, joyful stride into womanhood can become a fearful vacillation between risking the loss of a father and the desertion of a boyfriend. No wonder few women report sexual pleasure and orgasm as a result of the first act, so fraught with consequences imagined or real.

Both father and daughter require time to adjust to her new, nonvirgin status. For a while a daughter can successfully hide it from him. Normal privacy prevails. After all, she does not know about his sex life. Both prefer to think of the other as pure. Many children say they cannot imagine their parents engaging in sex. Eventually, however, it becomes evident that she is no longer a virgin. The fearful secret is out. A period of bewilderment may occur which may precipitate open combat or fearful withdrawal. She imagines her father is upset and wounded if he says nothing, and she may be right. Or she cowers from or bristles at his attack. Mutually, they mourn the loss of the special closeness they have had. Never again will it be the same. He must share her with another man.

The period of adjustment may take several years while yearning for the past continues, especially at times when a daughter experiences trouble with her husband or lovers. Many women regret their first few lovers; they feel they were tricked and abandoned. For them, the sex was timid, inhibited, and not much fun. Mourning the loss of their little-girl status with father, they found their new lovers sadly deficient in caring. Most women from stable families find no man will ever love them as their parents did. No nervous college undergraduate struggling to find his identity and place in the world will show the care and consideration showered on a woman by her male parent.

I have seen many more women tied to fathers who are too kind, generous, helpful, and charming than I have seen cut off by uncaring, abusive ones. Cared for emotionally and finan-cially by a doting and worldly father, the twenty-year-old girl may well find the uncertain, egocentric boy-men who are her first lovers to be dull company. Not only do their qualities pale by comparison, but keeping company with them may deprive her of the consistent attention she has been used to from her bright, lively, assured, and accomplished father. A father who allows himself to be flattered by his apparent suc-cess in the unequal competition with her young lovers and who strives to hold on to his daughter too much (some hold-ing on, after all, is only human) can prolong the period of psychological virginity.

Having taken the nervous step into adult life of first sexual intercourse, a step unsupported by her family and especially by her father, the young woman expects a lot from her young lover. Sometimes—too often—she looks for the same protec-tion and oasis that her father had given her. When her young lover becomes frightened of intense closeness at too early an age he may leave her or make demands on her that her father never would. Often a young woman, after a nervous sexual step or flurry of activity, enters into a second period of virgin-ity as she tries to restore the secure past of her childhood. Es-pecially when her father does not know about her sexual ex-perience, she may try to be accepted back by him as a virgin in an attempted return to the oasis period.

When the first man with whom she has had intercourse be-comes her husband or long-term lover, one of several things may happen. She may try to cling to him in order to simulate the comfortable time she had with her father. If the lover has similar needs, they may enter into a symbiotic relationship which leaves her fixed as a little girl. Such affairs become stormy after a while. Women who remain daddy's little girl, expecting lifelong status as children, fight a lot with their husbands and lovers but cannot rid themselves of these men.

First intercourse is a nervous, uncomfortable act for almost every woman; a necessary step into adulthood that is usually taken without parental support. A father and a daughter need several years to adjust to their new status with one another. He is no longer the most important man in her life. It is a loss which they both mourn. During her twenties, they adjust to their new adult separateness while continuing valued parts of their past. The process goes on for a decade; when it is complete, she becomes sexually mature.

LOSS OF PSYCHOLOGICAL VIRGINITY

Real loss of psychological virginity requires the abandonment of childlike attachments to parents, especially father. It is ironic that the very step into adult sexual independence invites regression. Sex takes place in a bed in which you are held, loved, excited, and hope to be pleased, fulfilled, and, finally, peaceful. The relief of tension is promised. Sexual intercourse provides an *adult oasis,* whose emotional origins come from the happy early years with father. When a young woman fully examines her sexual longings and desires, she realizes she hopes to return to the oasis in which she is unconditionally loved and accepted. How adult are these wishes? Very! All your life you retain the desire for an oasis, a place where you are cared for, where your tensions are relieved, where you are not judged and do not have to perform in order to be loved. Once, you had all this from your father.

The reason a woman looks for an emotional connection in addition to the physical one is the special closeness she once enjoyed with her father. The memory is indelibly imprinted on her emotions. If the longing is not satisfied at all, she feels an emptiness. Adult relationships which inadequately satisfy the need for closeness are unstable and upsetting to her. Because the oasis was a feature of early preverbal childhood, the memory of it is largely unarticulated. However, though a woman may not have words for her yearning, she can still feel it.

Obviously any relationship that combines physical and emotional closeness is a healthy and fulfilling one. It seems that many women sense the need for both kinds of intimacy more deeply and fully than do men. Some women might disparage immature desires for tenderness and bonding in an effort to mimic male sexuality, which is a more physically oriented sexuality. They may not realize that these are normal needs deriving from the oasis period. In fact, it is the natural yearning for emotional content in their sexual relationships that makes it easier for women than for men to achieve intimacy and emotional closeness.

Another pattern established during the oasis period, one which may prove damaging, is based on the fact that a little girl is used to being catered to and taken care of by her father. By transferring to sexual intercourse that kind of passivity, so that she only reacts to her lover's advances, a woman is unlikely to please her partner or herself.

Sexual intercourse is not like a mother's breast; it cannot unfailingly provide relief from discomfort. Nor is it like a father's unconditional love and care. Adults are not as simply satisfied as infants. What are the sources of a woman's sexual satisfactions? Having orgasms consistently, which may take two to five years to develop following first intercourse, is important but by itself not enough. Being held, admired, spoken to gently, and lingered over are even more important to most women. Repeatedly, researchers have found that a woman craves more than physical orgasm from a man. She wants feelings of affection and closeness, thus re-creating the special relationship she enjoyed as a little girl with her father.

Yet she must make some fundamental emotional changes in herself or she will fail to find sex a source of adult satisfaction. She will be disappointed if she expects the bed, without effort from her, to provide all that mother and father gave her as a little girl. If she remains a little girl psychologically, she will be angry with her lover and deprived of adult sexuality and its pleasures. Unsatisfied and resentful, she will turn away from men and seek satisfaction in other activities. By rejecting her lover and his provision of realistic adult comfort, the disappointed adult-child becomes preoccupied with her self, her comfort, her material acquisitions. These are the traits of narcissism, so frequently decried these days. Yet if women (and men, too) could modify their childhood longings, they would be able to settle happily for the gratifications that exist in the mature world.

What must the adult woman do about her continuing emotional need for a childlike oasis in order to find mature pleasure? A woman must first understand why she is dissatisfied with her lover. One reason why some women cannot communicate what pleases them to their partners is the result of a vestigial expectation from the oasis period; they assume their lovers will know and anticipate their sexual needs just as their fathers did their other needs. Yet many women remain dissatisfied even after they make their sexual needs known. Often it is because they are still unaware of the paternal influence present in their sexual encounters. Their mutual delight was a haven of security and comfort for both father and daughter. Taking refuge from a scary world, refuge offered by the dear older man, was essential for the little girl, and her development would have suffered if she had never known such love and attention from her father. She would delight much less in her adult male lovers if she had been deprived of the joys and reassurances of this period, for it was during these years that her capacity to love and be loved developed. These happy years were also her most impressionable, and they left her longing for a return to the oasis. The persistent yearning for one's parents and their care is heard in the deathbed cries of eighty- and ninety-year-olds as they call for their mothers and fathers. There is something of the child ineradicably present in all of us and a woman should not expect herself to surrender totally her youthful longings. But to become capable of mature love she must modify them radically.

Those who try to reestablish completely the embracing oasis of infancy face bleak fates. They are destined for angry disappointment and cynicism. Or in an incessant search for romance, they will rush from the ecstasy of new love to deep despair several months later when once again their childish expectations are unfulfilled. The cynics escape the painful depressions the romantics suffer after their rollercoaster flings, but the cynics are a bitter lot, ever angry at men.

There are women who, in an effort to manage their feelings and desires, err in the opposite direction. They relinquish all notions of a re-created childhood oasis so completely that they deliberately choose cold, ungiving lovers, leaving themselves in no danger of expecting too much or suffering disappointment. These women are forced into a meager adulthood, in which they must fend for themselves emotionally, because their chosen lovers supply little or nothing. The desire for regression is subdued by its object's being made too patently unobtainable.

Mature love requires abandoning the wish for a complete

oasis from adult responsibility and giving up the desire for relief of tension by mother's breast or father's care. *It means acceptance and enjoyment of pleasure through one's own efforts.* Instead of expecting to be excited and delighted passively by a tender, expert lover, a woman must learn to enjoy giving pleasure as much as receiving it. Such a woman is as happy about his orgasm as hers. Mature love also means benefiting from the adult-oasis aspect of sexual intercourse. Of course, even tender, loving sex with husband or partner will not make the cares of life disappear. While a child expects a parent to take *all* cares away, an adult woman would only expect her lover to supply a bit of escape and pleasure, allowing her to return to the realities and problems of life rested and cheered.

In order to enjoy fully the adult oasis of sexual intercourse a woman must feel fulfilled in other aspects of living. She must enjoy her career and/or her role as wife and mother, her friends, and her leisure. Relieved of excessive, immature expectations and prepared to participate actively in the giving and receiving of erotic pleasure, she will enjoy the physical and emotional bonding with her partner. Such pleasure will help her feel anchored in her life and at peace.

INCEST TABOO

All human societies have a rule prohibiting close relatives from having sexual relations with each other. The reasons for the universal law are the wish to know who fathers children, the need to limit dangerous rivalries within a family, and, in modern times, a deliberate effort to avoid genetic defects. The incest taboo prevents father and son from fighting over the woman who is daughter to one and sister to the other. Male relatives cooperate rather than compete. Incest rules serve to preserve the family.

In spite of rules, when male and female live together, desire is aroused. The underlying attraction between fathers and daughters is strong. The rule against expression of sexual feelings is observed in varying degrees from stiff, distant, untouching formality to warm kisses and caresses which can be dangerously arousing. This section will be concerned only with the observance of the taboo and not with incest itself.

The amount of erotic attraction between father and daughter and the extent to which the rule against revealing it is observed affects the young woman's sexual development. Most daughters are unaware of their overt libidinal feelings toward their fathers, although they may be quite conscious that their fathers are attractive. Near-violations of the incest rule by a father, such as talking suggestively, appearing nude, kissing, or erotically fondling, make a daughter uncomfortable and anxious rather than sexually aroused. Some young adolescent girls are even threatened by a chaste dance with their fathers and feel discomfort and vague disgust.

Some daughters are more attractive and naturally sexual with their fathers than other daughters. Without realizing it, a daughter might arouse her father, who, if he does not understand what is going on, may push her away in excessive alarm. Then, if he remains aloof, she regards him as cold and unfeeling. Since fathers are adults and supposed to have more control of their erotic feelings, the burden is placed on them rather than on their young daughters for maintaining a suitable equilibrium. It is important to remember that women have different levels of sexuality. One daughter may be more sexually stimulated by her father's caress than her less erotic sister.

There are a number of ways in which the incest taboo may affect a woman's life with her lover or husband. Having been raised by a father for whom she has incestuous feelings, she learns to defend herself from the stirrings of sex or to deny them altogether. If the attraction is recognized, she might feel disgust and anxiety, and withdraw herself. Or she might repress the feelings completely. Yet she loves and admires her father and searches for a man possessing his fine qualities. Finding such a man, she may discover unhappily that she has no sexual feelings for him. On the other hand, her initial erotic attraction may disappear once their relationship becomes long-term or legalized by marriage. The woman who loses her sexual desire whenever her love affairs become serious does so because she has been brought up under the incest taboo, in which sexual feelings toward members of the family are outlawed. In her case, once she becomes close to a man in or out of wedlock he begins to be a member of her family and her sexual desire for him must disappear. The incest taboo works even more quickly and automatically for some women. They are unable to feel erotic toward any man who shares their background, even though he qualifies in every other way as a candidate for spouse or serious lover. These women may only be attracted to men of exotic race or foreign nationality and indifferent to men more like themselves.

One young woman reported a predilection for exotic men, an inability to sustain a good sexual relationship, and an ardent attachment to her father. At first, she saw no connections among these facts; gradually, she acknowledged the influence of her father on her choice of lovers and the quality of her relationships. After further questioning, the exact nature of her father's effect upon her became clear to her.

There had been two recurrent patterns to her relationships. The more conventional and steady sort of affair was usually with a man who resembled her father in background and character. It typically began as an all-consuming romance which rapidly deteriorated into boredom and sexlessness. The other kind of affair was with exotic or married men whom she met for stolen days and hideaway weeks. She found it difficult to achieve orgasm consistently and was upset that any lover who initially appeared strong and promising inevitably soon proved weak and dependent.

She came to realize that she was motivated by incestuously inspired desires. Yet, more specifically, it was the incest taboo that was at work. The patient was attracted to men similar to her father in one of two ways. Either a man resembled her father in personality and attainment or, more dramatically, by being married or very exotic, shared her father's status—unavailability. Yet both kinds of men met a predictable fate because of the incest taboo. If a man had qualities similar to her father and was available, her sexual feelings would disappear because he was *too* reminiscent of her father. On the other hand, the exotic lover, much different from her father, enticed her with his unavailability.

As she learned to relate her powerful attraction to her father to her romantic history, the predictable patterns began to weaken. In time, she recognized that she had been unable to combine sex and love because of the incest taboo. With this self-awareness, she began to free herself from the tyranny of former choices and habits.

GUILT

If the lingering of psychological virginity from the late teens to early thirties (too often even beyond) diminishes sexual pleasure and intimacy with lovers, the prime reason for it is guilt. The irrational sense of having done something wrong, instilled through the years of childhood and adolescence, impoverishes a woman's erotic life.

All fathers imbue their daughters with sexual guilt to some extent, although the amount varies greatly. When women were asked which of their parents seemed more upset at the prospect of their loss of virginity, the majority responded their fathers. Many couldn't wait to tell their mothers after they had slept with someone, but they feared their fathers' discovery and often actively hid it from him.

Some fathers of women I interviewed exercised surveillance of their teenage daughters with the zeal of the FBI, snooping into darkened living rooms and parked cars, casing teenage bars and dance halls, almost insanely trying to discover their little girls engaging in sexual activity or to deter them from it. Such nervous fathers are not that rare. Daughters of such men have curious responses to the sleuthing. Some pick equally jealous lovers who haunt them in much the same way; others respond in the opposite fashion by choosing calm, trusting men. Oddly, the latter occasionally miss all the fuss about sex and almost crave the police drama that once surrounded their erotic lives. They may feel bored with their lovers' equanimity.

A lurking father investigating and protecting his daughter's chastity reflects an irrational apprehension about the impending loss of a daughter's virginity. However, such excessive worry is not only common, it also makes a lasting impression. A zealous paternal concern is transmitted to a sensitive young girl about to commit the first, secret, unsupported, even condemned act of sexual intercourse.

When questioned why they thought their fathers would be upset with the knowledge of their loss of virginity, daughters most frequently answered that their fathers, recalling how lustful they had been toward girls when they were adolescents, expected boys to behave equally badly with their daughters. As fathers, they wanted to protect their daughters from being hurt or used. I suspect that this answer, though common, is wrong. Why does a father become so troubled and often irrationally upset? It is because he is experiencing the loss of the oasis he and his little girl have shared, as she separates and gives herself to another. The sexual activity of most reasonably normal parents and their children is private. Most adolescents and young adults cannot imagine their parents having sex and most adults do not discuss the details of their sex lives with their offspring. Similarly, a young woman beginning to explore sex does not talk about it with her father. A secret therefore grows between them. Moreover, the adolescent and young adult woman becomes preoccupied with her lover and thus has less time and emotion for her father. While he doesn't sit down and analyze all that is taking place, a father experiences the threatened loss and reacts with the wish to prevent it.

In addition to feelings of separation and loss, there is the continued force of the Judaeo-Christian, puritan, antisex ethic, which regards women as pure, especially those in one's family, and most especially young unmarried daughters. A young woman wants to be pure for her father, for her minister, priest, or rabbi, for the man she loves, and for herself. At times she may almost be reassured by her father's efforts to restrain her sexual activities, since she herself is making a similar attempt.

Most fathers do not knowingly encourage sexual guilt in their daughters. They do it by acting upset if their daughters come home later than the early—sometimes excessively early

—hour they set as curfew. They do it by not allowing them to go to appropriate events such as dances or parties. They fuss excessively about chaperones. Unwittingly they instill sexual guilt by prohibiting their daughters from going out with older boys or boys deemed sexually aggressive. But they also do it by implying that they would be hurt or let down should their daughters sleep with someone. In fact, it was the reluctance to hurt their fathers that made the majority of women interviewed hide their sexual activity from their fathers. It certainly was not fear of their overt punishment or wrath. Some daughters reported yet another indirect inducement of guilt: it was the mother who said, "Your father will be very upset if you go out with" so and so or "go too far" with him.

The effect of a father's pressure on his daughter to refrain from intercourse is a leading cause of continuing psychological virginity, sexual guilt, and inhibition long after she, and often her father too, wish it would disappear. Frigidity and lack of sexual pleasure and orgasm with a suitable lover or husband is not something most fathers would wish on their daughters. The protection of the fifteen-year-old girl is not intended to destroy the sexual life of the thirty-five-year-old married woman. Both father and daughter were flustered and upset twenty years earlier but neither intended the result to be lifelong. Why then do these inhibitions persist? They persist because young persons are impressionable and nervous, and the powerful preoccupations of their fathers do not disappear. The force of long-ago mandates, no longer relevant, plagues the sexually inhibited adult.

Many women barely realize how much the paternal sexual attitude changes over the years. One Catholic woman in her late twenties remembered her father's stringent rules and strict enforcement of her teenage curfew. He warned her repeatedly not to trust men sexually. When she began to sleep with men at age twenty-five she found herself frightened and inhibited. As her erotic pleasure in bed slowly improved, she still suffered from guilt the day after making love. On her twenty-ninth birthday she went home and was having a late drink with her father after her mother had gone to bed. They began to talk about the men in whom she was currently interested. She found herself amazed that her father assumed she was sleeping with her lover. He had changed. She had not. She could still hear his prohibitions from her impressionable adolescence.

A daughter often does not notice that her father's attitude toward her sexual behavior changes as she advances into her twenties. Freud observed the timeless nature of the unconscious, in which events that happened long ago have the force of current reality. A father's initial nervousness about his little girl's loss of virginity carries much more force in her psyche than do the more lenient attitudes which he adopts after she becomes an adult. The battles they had during her adolescence, as he tried to hold his virgin daughter, leave their mark. Although she struggled to get away, part of her did not want to leave the oasis.

Fathers change. They do so as daughters grow older. Your father's current views may be unknown to you. Do not live under fifteen-year-old tyranny. You will be surprised to learn he now regards you as a sexual woman, not a little girl. Both of you have grown and developed. In general, societal attitudes about sex have become more liberated. It is possible your father has remained closed to your having become sexually mature, but you owe it to both of you to give him a chance. You may be in for a pleasant surprise.

FEAR OF DOMINANCE

Women do not want to be exploited by men either domestically or in the marketplace. Too many have seen their mothers become bitter. Although many women resist objectively and outwardly, they often remain unaware of their subjective, deeply psychological fear of men. They are unconscious of how intimacy with a man frightens them. Yet they experience the indirect effects of the dread by being unable to enjoy sex fully, by failing to combine sex with love, or by withdrawing from males. Often they are lonely, unable to sustain intimacy, or only capable of casual promiscuity. They may believe they are looking for a man, but in fact they are hiding.

Fathers usually have something to do with these women's fears. Weak fathers may make daughters fearful; for these women, mothers are powerful and men are children. Uninteresting male parents are unable to attract their daughters, providing them with no practice in relating to vigorous males. Autocratic fathers can also raise daughters who either fear or mimic male dominance; these women need weak lovers to push around. They don't respect their lovers and go from one to the next unhappily.

Case History: Weak Father, Frightened Daughter

Barbara Winters is a strong, stocky, assertive engineering student in her early twenties. Her mother, an advertising executive, constantly berates her about her weight. Barbara suspects that her weight makes her unattractive to strong, exciting men, men she would prefer to the timid and asexual ones with whom she has tortured, shy courtships without real lovemaking.

Her father is shy, quiet, and distant. They have never gone out for lunch together, shared an afternoon on the town, or taken any joint excursion. In fact, he has rarely spoken to Barbara since she reached puberty. He is a very successful man in the world of business, but he directs none of his energy or purpose to his daughter. Barbara cannot recall hearing any opinion of his firsthand.

It is her mother who speaks for the parents. "Your father thinks" this or "Your father feels" that frequently accompanies her pronouncements. In fact, Barbara's mother overwhelms her with talk. Eager to be the star parent, her mother serves as her confidante, strategist, and conscience. She counsels Barbara not to pursue boyfriends, but to wait for them to initiate. Any other behavior would be unfeminine. Her mother's message seems to be that it is all right to lead a man around by the nose, but only after marriage. Otherwise, a woman should hide her strength. Her mother, fashionably trim, implores Barbara to lose weight, with the implication that she could then make a real catch.

Barbara does not trust men. She has never had intercourse with one she truly cared for and she has never enjoyed an erotic experience. Instead, sex has been brief, nervous, guilt-ridden, and unfulfilling.

The men to whom she becomes close emotionally are practically virgins and generally impotent. She and they waltz around each other at a nervous distance. They stay up through the night, having long, adolescent arguments. She can talk until dawn with these men; she expects no physical closeness or intimacy of them.

Her present boyfriend is bright and attractive, yet he has

trouble expressing his emotions. He casually goes to bed with women he does not know well or care about, yet he avoids sex and intimacy with Barbara. After months of daily contact in school, she was amazed to hear him confess that he found her attractive.

Impressions

Barbara Winters is a powerhouse, but her aggression is all bound up in her insecurities. She is, in fact, only ten pounds overweight. Yet it is not so much her appearance-obsessed mother as her successful but distant and withdrawn father who has caused her difficulties with men. Her father has never shown any interest in Barbara nor given her the impression he found her attractive. As a result, she cannot expect any man to be attracted. Her slim mother's excessive scolding about her extra weight telegraphs a message of competitive defeat: Barbara cannot win her father nor can she find a man as good as he. By remaining overweight, Barbara accepted the verdict.

Lacking any practice with men because of her father's inaccessibility, Barbara talks to men as though they were her mother. This is the only warmth and intimacy for which she has been prepared. Real closeness with a man eludes her. For her, the best part of sex is in the talk which precedes the act. Typically, these conversations go on until dawn and serve to calm her distress about feeling unattractive to all except perhaps her mother, with whom she has similarly long dialogues about her relationships.

Simulating her own family life, she chooses weak men she would need to lead, but does not assert herself because it would be unfeminine. Understandably, she is angry at and disappointed in men. Her present boyfriend is a frightened man who does not communicate his feelings. Just like her father, he disappoints her.

Barbara has a strong mother and an essentially absent father. Her boyfriends are either impotent or frightened. The result is no sex. With her dozen lovers of one or two nights' duration, sexual intercourse gave no pleasure. Her occasional indulgence in excessive drinking with loss of control, followed by inebriated pursuit of her impotent and timid boyfriends, represents an unconscious wish to reach her father.

Recently, Barbara has begun talking to her father about her monetary needs following graduation. Their conversations last an hour on the telephone. It is not an unreasonable thing for her to do with this successful businessman. Barbara is delighted to be talking to her father and consulting him. As she allows her father to assert his expertise and resists her mother's efforts to monopolize her, her relationships with men have begun to improve. She is also losing weight rapidly, but keeping that a secret from her parents.

Case History: Strong Father, Frightened Daughter

Nancy Chase is in her early thirties, unmarried, undated, and so lonely that she is barely able to hide it. She overworks, pursues too many hobbies, watches television during all her free time, and does anything she can to escape depression.

Her father is a wealthy, world-renowned industrialist. When she was young he paid enough attention to his bright daughter to stimulate and shape her interests. Yet he encouraged only those abilities he cared about, often ignoring the ones Nancy favored. Consequently, she is a stockbroker, a field of which he approves; she does very good work and enjoys none of it.

She recites a litany of resentments. She deplores her father's arrogant, bossy ways, his need to be right always, and his lack of interest in anyone but himself. She remembers him as selfishly trying to control her rather than promoting her individuality when she was young. She believed he favored her younger sister. As a teenager, Nancy was upset with several of her teachers, who treated her obsequiously because she was *his* daughter.

Her mother is always subservient and seldom speaks in her husband's presence. Nancy feels that her mother seems unable to relax easily. The only time she enjoys herself is when her husband is not around. Nancy's mother does nothing to protect or shield her daughter from her husband's control.

Nancy's love life has brought her no pleasure. She has never gone out with the bright, earnest, ambitious office boys destined to be company presidents, but she has dated instead men who were less intelligent, not motivated, weaker, and younger than she.

Impressions

Nancy has always been able to catalogue her father's faults. He is vain, selfish, overbearing, and opinionated. She feels burdened by his exalted standards. What Nancy has been reluctant to admit is the ways in which she is like her father. Even more difficult for her to acknowledge are her father's strengths and her own similarly strong qualities.

His mind so excited her as a little girl that as an adult she has been bored, except when she used her gifts in the way she had with him, under his direction. She wants to be rich, just like her father, but she wants to be recognized for herself, for her own potential and achievement, not for being the daughter of her father the success. Nancy cannot tolerate many of the traits she sees in her father and at the same time cannot recognize that she shares precisely those characteristics. Like him she is impatient, easily bored, driven to accomplishment, and avid for recognition.

Nancy's timid rebellion against her father has wasted her very considerable talents. Her choice of career was halfway between what each of them wanted for her, satisfying to neither. Her love life has similarly been compromised: her relationships to men have been hurt by the unresolved feelings she has toward her father. She turned to unsuitable men who hurt and used her, and finally has retreated into total isolation. Her feelings have been further confused and her resentment compounded by her mother's helplessness in dealing with her father's arrogance.

This gifted woman has begun to see that in fighting blindly against her dictatorial but fascinating father she has harmed her work and her emotional life. It is to be hoped that this intelligent and serious woman will be able to concede that she would be better off with a man more or less like her father—gifted, earnest, and ambitious—rather than the somewhat prosaic and undriven types with whom she has always consorted. Perhaps as she gains deeper self-knowledge she will also take firmer hold of her career.

HATRED OF MEN

While not always as strong as hatred, the lesser negative feelings of resentment, bitterness, and anger can also poison a woman's sex life. She may experience the results of these emotions without realizing the cause. Unwillingness to open up, loneliness, lack of orgasm, repeated breakups with lovers, can all come from deep-rooted anger. After a series of disastrous affairs she may feel justified in her resentment due to the men's repeated desertions rather than understand that her own anger may have caused her to drive them away, however unwittingly.

There is some anger in all of us from childhood, as we must be repeatedly frustrated while growing up because we can't have all we want. Parents must discipline and thus deny, sometimes in the child's interest and sometimes in their own interest. A father must release or maybe even expel his daughter from the childhood oasis, reducing his own delighted, uncritical involvement. He expects good performance and behavior in its place. Even the best of fathers can anger their daughters, while the worst can do damage by indifference or by paying court too assiduously.

When a father deserts his family or is abusive, his daughter's resulting anger may give her trouble with men all her life. She may totally avoid men, or keep seeking the father she never had. Women whose fathers have deserted them feel confused about how they are supposed to act with men, since they lost their means of practice. Others try to make up for the past deprivation in the present.

One woman in her mid-twenties, whose father had deserted her mother before she was born, boasted that none of her lovers ever cheated. Although she had once feared betrayal, she believed she had conquered her excessive jealousy. Yet the scar of her father's desertion remained. She watched her lovers closely to make sure they would not leave. She flew into a rage when her lover expressed the slightest interest in another woman at a party. Her deep anger toward and distrust of men had been encouraged by her bitter, lonely mother. As long as a new lover seemed completely devoted and under her control all was well, but as soon as he showed even the mildest interest in another woman her underlying terror and fury quickly ignited.

Once aroused, her strong possessiveness and deep anger destroyed one love affair after another. After several months, each relationship would deteriorate as her lover was driven away by her excessive demands. Her disappointment and resentment overwhelmed her erotic feelings. She would become unable to have an orgasm or feel sexual attraction. Soon the relationship would be over and she would go off searching for someone else to fill the void left by her father long ago.

Because she was lively, and attractive, she had little trouble in finding another man with whom to begin again. She suffered little depression because of her ability to restore her loss with someone new and devoted. The sexual excitement and romantic attention of a devoted lover made her quickly forget her recent disappointment and resentment.

Yet there is danger in store for a woman saddled with such anger. The toll for harboring ever-increasing bitterness and wrath is high. Consider the examples of two older women. The first woman is thin, brunette, very attractive, fifty-nine years old, and so toned by exercise and dieting that she looks years younger. She has used men for excitement and as an antidepressant and has had many affairs before, during, and after marriage.

Her father died when she was five. Now penniless and thrice divorced, she feels abandoned and hopeless, yet she is secretly proud of her ability to survive on her own. At the same time, she longs for a man to advise, guide, and take care of her, but she adamantly refuses to listen when she finds one. She is very critical and believes that "all men would walk out the door if they knew all the bad things I thought about them."

This woman is trapped by her personal history; she started and is ending a half orphan. Not having had a father since she was a baby, she has never learned to deal effectively with a man in order to get what she wants. Normally, a daughter learns when to use guile, direct honesty, charm, firmness, and anger in exchanges with her father. But this woman had had no such experience; she could only use her good looks to deal with men. To make her appearance even better, she went to spas and beauticians and wore expensive clothes. Indeed, she did attract men, but she always came away disappointed, because she did not know how to negotiate with them. They slept with her, gave her nothing, and left. Her anger at this sequence helped drive them away.

The second woman, in her sixties, is much angrier. Her father deserted his family when she was quite young, leaving her mother to bring up the children with very little money. The patient's childish anger and hurt have persisted to the present. When she was ten and starved for male affection, an older man took advantage of her and sexually fondled her. She regards this memory as another good reason to hate men. In addition, her ex-husband and several lovers have been dictatorial and high-handed. So she goes through life making a collection of cases and stories of harm inflicted on her and other women by arrogant and unfeeling men. At the same time she bitterly resents the falling off in attention she gets from men now that her beauty, which was outstanding in her youth, is fading. She is lonely, and she is angry in her loneliness. She knows that the only way for her to find and enjoy rewarding male companionship is to hate men less, but she cannot do so until she overcomes what she now regards as her well-justified belief that all men will only want to exploit and then desert her.

The departure of the father frequently does obvious damage to the daughter's life. Less evident deprivations also have consequences. Fathers who are absent, cruel, insensitive, unsupportive, who hurt or abuse in large or small ways, leave scars which are hard for their daughters to erase. Unpleasant memories and impressions can harm a daughter's sex life because they limit her capacity to trust and enjoy men. The legacy of anger left by an inadequate father can poison every aspect of the adult sexual relationship. To feel sexual desire for her lover a woman cannot be too angry at him or at men in general. A little irritation can be dissolved by intercourse, but deep unresolved hatreds destroy sex sooner or later. On the other hand, a woman who has made peace with the first man in her life, her father, a woman who has enjoyed his strengths and forgiven his faults, can reduce her anger and have a fulfilling adult love life.

PASSION OR CONTROL

Sex is an appetite and some women are hungrier than others. Degrees of desire are determined by constitutional factors and by upbringing. In Victorian times, when women were supposed to be pure and not to enjoy sex, most of them did not. The modern, contraceptively protected woman expects sexual pleasure, but she usually reserves it for the "right" person. Thus, her passion must be measured and held in check for the appropriate time and partner. She must know both control and release. Tight reins are kept on strong feelings and sometimes she has trouble letting go. Because of the need to combine sensuality with restraint, modern fathers and daughters are understandably confused about how a young woman can develop into a sometimes subdued, sometimes responsive adult. Passionate at the wrong moment, she risks indiscretion, promiscuity, adultery; constantly inhibited, she will be frigid and anorgasmic, and miss one of life's greatest pleasures.

In an age dominated by psychology, constitutional factors should not be forgotten. Some women have more sexual drive than others. Young girls who are extremely sensual behave differently with their fathers than the daughters who are more restrained. A father may accept and handle a less sexual daughter easily, while being frightened by a second who is more openly sensual.

In spite of hormonal and hereditary variance, environment has the strongest impact on a woman's sexual drive and pre-occupation. The greatest source of environmental influence comes from a woman's father. Women who do not receive some infusion of sexual electricity from their fathers as they grow up are, on the average, cooler and less passionately sexual than those who do.

Many women describe their fathers as cold, aloof, uncommunicative, even absent, and therefore wonder how I can refer to any sexual electricity coming from these distant figures. But the reported degree of paternal emotional distance is often exaggerated by a daughter to protect herself from the knowledge of her father's sexuality. Many daughters cannot acknowledge erotic feelings between their fathers and themselves.

A father's sexual fantasies and behavior affect his daughter no matter what form they take. A daughter learns about his eroticism by watching his behavior with herself and other females, by listening to his stories about his experiences with women and by whatever her mother tells her. She learns about the strength of his sexual drive and its direction. She finds out what he really believes about acceptable sensuality in life, whether it should be passionate and important or restricted and careful.

A bright, attractive, twenty-six-year-old financial analyst has a history of one brief marriage and many failed relationships with men. Repeatedly, she has moved from overinvolvement to boredom and disappointment.

Her father is a rich, handsome philanderer, irresponsible and bored. When traveling in Europe she discovered him at a hotel with his mistress. Even his daughter's girlfriends at college were not immune to his aggressive charm. She found his successes with them to be particularly traumatic, and is profoundly distressed by all his womanizing.

Nevertheless she is fascinated and amused by his charm; his legacy is her pronounced inability to live a life of commonplace satisfactions. Steady, solid men bore her and she can barely stand those with social backgrounds like her own. On the other hand, she is excited by out-of-the-ordinary men such as musicians and writers. For their part, her exotic lovers at first work too hard to impress and win, then they weary and reject her. She winds up hurt and immediately goes on to the next affair.

Following her father's example, she took several lovers during a brief marriage while her staid, somewhat dull husband remained faithful. She so wanted to be like her father that she even had fantasies of seducing women.

This woman is too passionate and has been overstimulated by her father. If she finds a male colleague attractive, she sleeps with him. Her love life is a series of affairs each starting with passion, followed by quick cooling and breaking up. She has a need for excitement and is unable to stand a calm, steady life. Those who are addicted to passion are like those who need the aid of drugs or alcohol to make their existence bearable.

If fathers can overstimulate, then they can certainly under-stimulate too. In fact, understimulation by the male parent appears to be more common than overstimulation. Since his mother was probably reared in the Victorian era and he him-self strongly wishes his daughter to be pure, a father may try to downplay the sexual aspects of his relation to her. If this is a sham she will see through it. However, if it is real she will lose her chance of trying out on him her growing sexuality. A cold, relatively sexless woman will result.

A young woman may unfairly blame her father for her sex-ual problems. Controlling passion, confining it to the right time and place, is hard for her. She is tempted to blame her difficulties on her father. As a woman matures into her twen-ties and beyond, she begins to appreciate the difficulty of her father's role with her as she developed. She understands bet-ter his wish for her to enjoy mature, loving sex and to avoid being hurt by indiscriminate affairs with ill-chosen partners. As the adult daughter forgives her father she learns to relax more with her lover and becomes increasingly adept at mix-ing control and passion.

Women naturally vary in sexual aggressiveness, from those who wait for their lovers to take full lead to those who ac-tively seduce their men. A woman's behavior is largely influenced by her father and how much he encouraged her as-sertiveness in general and whether he wanted her to be pas-sive and pliable or not.

HEALTHY SEXUAL INTIMACY

A woman's ability to achieve enjoyable, lasting, intimate sex-ual relations with her lover requires healthy resolution of the issues I have discussed. True loss of virginity, relative absence of sexual guilt, a proper perspective on the incest taboo, little or no fear of or anger toward men, a healthy capacity for passion, and a comfortable balance between assertiveness and passivity are needed. A woman needs either to have had a close enough relationship with her father to stimulate her femininity and allow her to practice it on him or a chance to think about and work out any conflicts caused by paternal deprivations in her childhood. Humans have ample flexibility and powers of recovery, enabling them to cure even severe impairments from their youth.

Very few women have had ideal relationships with their fathers. Sexual problems are common. Yet most sexual difficulties can be overcome as a woman gains experience and understanding, especially understanding of the influence of her father on her erotic life.

Three

CAREERS

For a woman to live in a manner for which she has not been raised, to act in ways never observed or practiced in childhood, is not easy. The examples set by her parents often do not serve to guide her career path. Mother labored in the kitchen and father's job was unseen. The growing girl did not witness careers. Instead they have been papered over by magazines' views of the working woman. Females are going into the labor force and they do not know how to behave because many of their mothers were not career women. The lucky ones have had visible and interested fathers, but the majority of women do not know how assertive to be, when to speak or listen, whether to be strong adults or pretty girls, how to handle sexual attractions and offers, whether it is all right to raise their voices with emotion or even to cry. They do not know if they will be appreciated and promoted because of

their competence and intelligence or because of how they relate to important members of the company organization.

Books and magazines tell women how to behave, how to
dress for success, how to form a network, the importance of
mentors, how to handle sexual advances, the degree of
assertiveness, how to combine competence and femininity,
and how to mix all of this with marriage and motherhood.

Boys and girls build their notions of their sex roles from experiences with *both* sexes. From these they learn what they
are not, what they can never be, what they wish they were,
and what they might become. Usually it is what her father
gave her that affects the way a woman enters the work world
more than her mother's influence, although the latter is also
very important. There are two ways that father's influence ex-
erts itself on his daughter's career.

The first concerns the level of development she has
achieved and the degree to which she has separated from
him. The oasis child has little ambition in business. She
remains father's little girl and not too different from her
homebound mother. The adolescent belongs neither to him
nor to the world of work but vacillates in between, filled with
conflict. The mature woman whose father helped her become
grown-up and independent is ready for a career, but not completely. The reason is that even she is a navigator in un-
charted waters. A childish aspect of a mature woman's anger
toward her father concerns the wish that he had shown the
way, prepared her to be an executive, to know what to do.
Perhaps your father did instruct his sons better than you, but
it was because women's roles are changing and he had no
idea of what you would be facing.

Nonetheless, the second way a father influences his daughter's career concerns the way he perceives and encourages her
and the example he sets. Fathers have different expectations

for daughters and sons, but also from one daughter to another. Some are expected to be pretty housewives and others, lawyers. These attitudes are not always or entirely capricious but can be based on the perceived abilities, appearances, and temperaments of the young women. What is unfortunate is erroneous, premature predictions that do not give the developing girl a fair chance. Snap judgments by fathers amount to prejudice, assessing the young person too soon, forgetting that children develop at different rates. Also, there is a tendency to disregard women with less than dazzling elementary and high school records as destined to be cared for like children by husbands. Sons of less than top scholastic ability are still expected to make their own way in the world and not just to marry.

Research has shown that father's influence on his daughter's career is usually less ambivalent and therefore healthier than it is on her sex life. The average father wants his daughter to do well in school, to have a good, well-paying job, and feels proud when she advances. His only reservation concerns marriage and children, and he may place these first. So may she. A selfish father promotes what he wants in spite of his daughter's wishes, while a supportive and generous one helps her decide or goes along with her independent decision.

A father's influence on his daughter's career is determined by how he relates, what he expects, and whether he instructs. Warm fathers with low expectations influence their females far differently from warm fathers with high expectations who show the woman how to enter and be successful in a career. Male parents with high expectations who are cold and do not instruct often produce ambitious, frustrated, and angry daughters, furious that the world does not recognize them but unable to make their own way.

WORK AND ITS PROBLEMS

Being prepared for the world of work means being ready for its problems. These include three aspects: entering, being judged, and getting ahead. Entering a career is a major transition from childhood to adulthood. Instead of being given to, a young woman begins to get for herself. Growing up can be described as a transition from an *af*fective to an *ef*fective state, in which the former involves the feeling state of the impotent child happy when given to, angry and sad when deprived, while the latter encompasses the ability of the adult to control her destiny and effect change. Whether a woman enters the world of work psychologically on a child, adolescent, or adult level will strongly affect the course of her career. Her father influences her start by the degree to which he has helped her mature and by his instructions and expectations. He may oppose her having a career or find her her first job, advise wisely or offer unrealistic suggestions, be totally uninterested or too involved, and all of these will affect her at a delicate moment—the beginning of her working life.

In her new career a woman is open to judgment and criticism. The more childlike and insecure ones find this very hard to take. Because many women are first-generation workers whose mothers are housewives, they are unsure of themselves and more upset by criticism than men. The girl who is a reluctant refugee from the childlike oasis she shared with her adoring father is little prepared for the negative comments of her male boss who is her father's age. She finds in general that people are not as supportive at work as they were at home. Of course, no one gets to adulthood and her first job without having heard criticism from teachers, friends, enemies, mothers, siblings, or classmates, even if she had a doting father. But the woman who pioneers new career territory is nervous, insecure, and not very open even to constructive criticism. A *Wall Street Journal* piece in 1979 found male supervisors aware of this and reluctant to criticize female underlings with the same candor as male subordinates. Mature women who make it to the top overcome this tendency if they have it and accept censure. Neither men nor women like criticism but there is no way to avoid it.

Many factors influence whether a woman advances in her job. Motivation, talent, political sense, and mind style—all are important. Motivation comes from within and without, from the desire to prove herself or to measure up to an internalized ideal, to an original parental expectation that now has become her own goal and from the push and shove of others outside, from friends, competitors, siblings, and parents. The desire to get ahead can be perverse, to show a father up, to prove him wrong, that his view of her as only pretty, as merely marriage material, is incorrect. The more forceful and dogmatic, the more authoritarian a father, the more likely a daughter will strongly react for or against, give in or fight his wishes.

Once motivated, a woman must channel and harness her talent, give up her role as little girl, close off her universe of options in the effort to develop a few skills, to become professional, respected for ability. Often women are brought up to be lovable, to please rather than to be competent and strong. Instead of charming the organization, she must learn to be compatible with the network, to get it to help her achieve her goals. Getting ahead requires the initial ability to conform, to follow the rules of the organization enough to be trusted and accepted, to then get into a position of leadership, to be able to set the rules. Women like men can be neither too docile and conforming nor rebellious and difficult. Women whose spirits have been broken by dictatorial fathers, who are unable to function unless ordered, will rarely make it to the top, nor will those who have become so rebellious and antiauthority against strong fathers that they fight their bosses and organization so much they cannot be accepted. Being truly successful is difficult and rare for both men and women. Required is a combination of talent, confidence, interpersonal skill, and strong motivation. Women certainly have the talent, but their interpersonal skills while remarkable in ability to get along are often not used politically to get ahead. It is one thing to be sensitive and another to use one's capacity to handle people in order to achieve one's goals. Women's confidence and motivation are often underdeveloped or lacking because of how they are brought up. As the career woman and female executive becomes more accepted and routine this will no doubt change.

MIND STYLES

The styles of women's minds can be viewed according to their fields of excellence, degree of originality, strength, and kindness. Excellence is a matter of attitude and of specialty. The female dilettante of the drawing room may be delightful, but she is not an expert, a paid professional called upon to complete important tasks. Much attention is being currently given to women and mathematics, since fear and failure in this area deprives women of entrance into medicine, physics, chemistry, engineering, architecture, economics, the financial sphere, and the serious world of money even as it pertains to marriage and self-sufficiency. There is no reason why women cannot be good at numbers and mathematical reasoning other than a vestige of sex-role stereotype.

Styles of minds vary from originality to conformity. The idea that men pioneer new thoughts and businesses while women maintain them, that men's minds are original while women's conform, that men are brilliant and restless while women are good at details and routine, that men are entrepreneurs and women secretaries, is unfortunately widespread.

In order for women to have a real chance for lively and interesting careers male bosses must change their attitudes toward them. Women must present themselves as original leaders, not docile followers. Unfortunately, some fathers share the attitudes of male managers and prefer their daughters as caretakers rather than as executives. If your father has not encouraged you to use your mind and talent to its fullest, you may automatically fulfill a subordinate role unless you stop and think what has happened to you. Sometimes it is not your father but your mother who has discouraged you, perhaps because she is jealous that you will have a better, freer life than she did or perhaps because she honestly would prefer you to give her grandchildren, not new corporate structures. Sons are brought up with one goal in mind, success, whereas daughters are expected to divide their efforts between career and children. For a woman to be original requires strength, confidence in her own thinking power, a willingness to stand up to questioning and even attack, and the courage to query the conventional wisdom and try something new.

THE MALE AND FEMALE PRINCIPLE IN BUSINESS

If men are noted for courage, restlessness, and originality, then women are seen as nurturing, pleasing, and selfless. It is important not to downgrade the latter, since nurture and kindness are as important as excellence to a business organization. Business which is efficient yet inhuman may succeed for a while, yet ultimately will fail.

FATHER'S TWO MESSAGES

Father gives only one message to his son—succeed—but to his daughter it is one of three: career, motherhood, or both. The minority who encourage their female offspring to remain childless and work produce high achievers who pursue their careers with little hesitancy. Those who encourage motherhood and view work as unnecessary or unimportant are most likely to have oasis girls with little career ambition. They may function contentedly in a low-level position, while seeking a husband with whom to have a baby. But more and more fathers want their daughters to combine career and family life.

The two instructions most fathers give have doubled their daughters' problems. While it is completely desirable for women to experience the satisfaction, self-expression, and sense of accomplishment from a meaningful career, plus the self-reliance that comes from having money of their own, it has also placed an excessive burden on them. Most fathers have no idea how their little girls can become superwomen, successful at fifty- to seventy-hour-a-week careers, and good mothers who are there to meet the needs of their babies. Many women are angry at their fathers for unthinkingly having encouraged this impossible dual role. Their anger frequently spills over onto their boss (whether female or male) and also onto the organization. Women who try for combined perfection in career and motherhood usually feel deficient in one or the other if not both. They become angry, confused, feel ineffective, unable to perform well, and it often hurts their careers.

JOB AND MATURITY

The Child

Grown women who remain children psychologically are severely hampered in their careers. Angry over the lost oasis shared with father, seeking it again as adults only to be frustrated and disappointed, the best they can hope for is a benevolent boss to whom they play loyal little girl. She calls him Mister and he calls her by her first name. Twenty-five years ago, a woman could function more contentedly in this setting, but nowadays she wants to be more independent, highly paid, and responsible. One reason is that her sisters are spontaneously treated as equals or, if not, demand to be dealt with as such. She is influenced by their attitudes and by their accomplishments. The oasis girl cannot re-create her protected childhood as an adult, but whenever she tries she feels uncomfortable because she observes the grown-up women around her.

Joyce Levine is thirty-three years old, unmarried, lonely, and angry. She was a virgin until her late twenties, and her love affairs have been disasters. Selfish, single, and mean married men have used and discarded her. For solace and refueling she still goes home to her parents.

Her jobs bring her no pleasure and are interrupted by long periods of loafing, sometimes accompanied by depression. Although it is twelve years since her first full-time employment and she is a college graduate, she has acquired no specific skills other than being a bank teller. Her male bosses like her because she is attractive, well dressed, has a sense of humor, and is conscientious.

Joyce is too frightened to work her way up in the world of advertising in which she has always been interested. She wanted to become a writer of television ads, but abandoned the idea when a girlfriend described the Madison Avenue world as too tough and competitive.

Occasionally she would go to a dinner party given by a female friend for a few women and become upset by their accomplishments. They all seemed to be bank vice-presidents, advertising executives, lawyers. No matter how good her job, she felt ashamed, ceased enjoying it, and quit. Executive women in the organization upset her the most. She hated their competence and assertiveness and could not stand being told what to do by them.

She thought about and made several more tentative gestures toward establishing a career for herself. She considered going to business school but shrank away. She took another job as a teller, which she hated from the start.

Her father is a bossy, extremely wealthy Long Island self-made real-estate tycoon who took all his sons into the business and has always been generous with his daughters. Thus, he has bound all his children to him emotionally and economically. Joyce's mother waits on him and follows his lead contentedly. Joyce is the youngest of his girls and remains his favorite, in spite of rebelling and giving him much cause for worry. He manages her well because he has catered to upset women in his family since childhood. In fact she is unconsciously fulfilling his need to be a caretaker and reminds him of his mother.

Joyce is the only one of his eight children who lives more than fifteen miles from him. While this is a source of pride to her, she remains financially dependent on him, even when working. Her father is not only wealthy, he sits on philanthropic boards, is a community leader respected for his common sense and ability to negotiate the most difficult situations. Although there has been considerable strife between them, he has remained number one in her affections. Her lovers have been married and clearly dallying or available but so inferior that she could not be serious about them. Her attachment to her father remains.

In spite of her continuing to be stuck psychologically as his little girl, their relationship has changed during her twenties and thirties. In the past, they fought intensely and any suggestion that she was in any way like him would enrage her. Now, she still dislikes his authoritarian, rigid, opinionated ways but can admire his trustworthy, kind, and skillful qualities. Rather than totally rejecting any similarity between them, she hopes to emulate his positive characteristics: confidence, success, courage, and leadership. In the past she responded mainly to his power, either giving in and trying to please or rebelling in the hope of getting away. His overpowering leadership left her feeling inadequate to stand on her own, to speak in class, to be independently competent in a career, or to believe she could interest a man.

Her attempt to separate from him in her twenties was harmed by his powerful control. He wanted her to be his kind of person: religious, submissive, good, and available to him. This left her passive and lacking in self-confidence. Father happily stepped into the very breach he created and encouraged, bossed, and ran her life. She fled to another city after having been graduated from college, but the geographical distance did not repair the emotional damage. She was unable to thrive on her own.

Her efforts at independence were difficult but very slowly productive. Hard won gains would disappear, forcing her to return to her ever-helpful father for necessary financial and emotional repair. Years slipped past. The story has a partially happy ending. She never made the step to an adult, independent, executive woman capable of leadership and risk, but, she found another brilliant man to work for, and she became his personal assistant. Having this kind, capable boss all to herself, she stopped worrying that she was only his secretary. He helped her esteem by teaching her about his business deals. She became very important to him and his dependence made her feel needed. She had made the best adjustment a child-woman can without growing. She accepted and became content. The fierceness of her father had fixed her level of development for life, but she was finally able to accommodate more happily.

The oasis girl in her twenties can be happy in a fairly undemanding job while she looks for a husband. Her lack of growth, which may present no problem during the twenty years in which she brings up her own children, may become one in her forties when she is faced with an empty nest and the need to do something constructive with the rest of her life. Oasis girls who do not marry but remain in subordinate positions have sometimes been able to find lifelong security and happiness with the right employer. But many become bitter because they are not challenged, their talents unused, salaries low, and needs for accomplishment unmet. Educated women who desire money and a sense of purpose are not content in the career of a secure, obedient child. These women want to innovate, not follow, to advance to greater responsibility and to earn a large salary.

The Adolescent

No one ever entirely grows up. We retain varying amounts of the good and bad of each decade, the wonder and negativism of childhood, along with the sensitivity and rebellion of adolescence. All of us have large reservoirs of the teenager, which on the positive side aids our creativity, philosophical thought, idealism, and concern over the oppressed, and on the negative detracts from our efforts because of moodiness, impatience, self-centeredness, restlessness, discontent, and boredom. But an adult who possesses some childlike and adolescent qualities is very different from one who never has grown up and remains fixated at a previous stage.

The main adolescent characteristics which harm a woman's career are difficulties with authority, the regulation of emotions, too much egocentrism, and conflicts between independence and dependence.

A woman who has too much teenager in her adult psyche will have problems with authority wherever she works. If she is in middle management, where conforming to company policy is required, she will constantly be fighting against it. She will find it so difficult to do what she is told that she may be unable to work in an organization at all. Authority conflicts in adolescent-like women make them unable to accept limits, to hear the boss say no, while at the same time they are unable to say no to their own subordinates. They cannot say no because they expect those under them to be as upset by hearing it as they are when it is said to them.

Adolescent-stuck women with authority problems are also unable to accept criticism. They feel angry and resentful and experience the desire for revenge, or begin to doubt their own worth. Their superiors find it very difficult to direct or correct them and find it nearly impossible to get them to do what is needed.

Teenage girls are moody and their emotions stormy. They rage easily, cry readily, are easily bored and restless, and have trouble containing their sexual impulses. All of these emotions must be properly regulated in order for a woman to succeed in a career. She cannot get angry too easily or extremely, but must control such feelings and express them at appropriate times and in useful ways. Boredom must be tolerated and restlessness overcome in any job. It is the patient who win out in careers, not those who change jobs too readily because they lose interest or who are so restless they cannot remain at a desk.

Sex for women in careers is a problem that has received widespread attention from the point of view of their being victimized by male superiors, but it also is a problem for young, sexy women to control this drive at work. Coming into close daily contact with attractive male peers and executives can be associated with strong erotic urges, which are almost always unwise to act upon. The ability to keep these more or less gracefully suppressed, not becoming cold or frightened around the desirable man, yet not having an affair with him, requires the capacity to maturely accept sensual desires, rather than being overwhelmed by them, whether deliberately or impulsively.

The excessive egocentrism of the adolescent makes her relatively unable to recognize the rights and needs of others. She feels entitled to recognition and special privileges and becomes enraged when they are not forthcoming. How dare her boss say no to something she wants to do? Not paying attention to other people, she alienates them and is unable to get them to do her bidding.

A main characteristic of the teenage years is the conflict between independence and dependence. At one moment a free-standing adult and at the next a dependent child, the adolescent goes back and forth between extremes. The career woman who is stuck at this level finds herself in the awful dilemma of being unwilling to follow directions and unable to give them. In an organization she may find a place in middle management where she can imagine she is self-sufficient, but in reality relies on her boss for security and direction.

Some women with severe adolescent conflicts are unable to work in organizations at all and instead function as free-lancers. If their problems are not too severe this can be a solution for them. For those who are stuck in their vacillation between dependence and independence, they find the need to be self-starting, which the self-employed must possess, overwhelming. They start projects they cannot finish. But those who grow outside the context of nine to five can become fully mature and successful working for themselves.

Amanda Roosevelt's career illustrates a journey from the negative aspects of adolescent influences on career to more positive ones. Amanda's father loved women and had many affairs during his long marriage. Her childhood oasis had been filled with his flirtatiousness and in her teens he continued to behave erotically around her, although there was no overt incest. His overstimulation left its mark by making her seek sexual excitement everywhere, including in her career. She would become the assistant of a brooding, creative filmmaker, fall in love, totally merge their existences, and live in this fantasy until the relationship terminated. The men for whom she labored were self-centered, complicated, difficult, and cruel. These were no eight-hour-a-day jobs, but total involvements of mind and body. Extreme emotion and adolescent instability would soon break them apart.

Because experience teaches, not everyone needs therapy.

Teenagers, however, are difficult to treat psychotherapeutically because they are not yet aware of the repetition compulsion and repeating patterns. Amanda began to notice the patterns without professional help. She could hardly miss them because what she was doing was extreme and painful.

She realized that if she could stop becoming sexually involved with her bosses and limit the length and intensity of her work day, she could still enjoy her job and be creative. She went to work in advertising, finding an outlet for her creative desires without the explosiveness of sex. It worked out very well. She made her positive adolescent traits work, while eliminating those that were hurting her career.

Some women are not so fortunate and continue to damage their careers because of negative, adolescent aspects of their personalities. Fearing authority and confinement, they struggle away in lonely, low-paying freelance efforts. Or they may continue at some seemingly glamorous task lured by the fantasied trappings of the work, but accepting poor pay or little hope for advancement.

The Adult

The woman whose father has helped her grow up and separate from him is ready to be mature about her career. She has developed the ego strength to be effective. Freud defined the ego as that part of the mind which is aware of reality, stores up experiences (in the memory), avoids excessively strong stimuli (through flight), deals with moderate stimuli (through adaptation), and causes changes in the external world to its own advantage (through activity). The ego also controls the emotions by deciding which are allowed satisfaction and under what conditions.

In order for a woman to be successful in her chosen career,

whether it be in an organization, freelance, or as an entrepreneur, she must possess the ego strength to deal with the outer world and with her own needs. Whatever her specialty, she must effectively interact with superiors, peers, subordinates, customers, or clients to her own advantage and where possible to theirs. She must be aware of nuances, remember the essential, adapt to gradual change or sudden surprise, and alter the situation for her own benefit wherever possible. She must express herself effectively, appropriately, and with necessary aggression, compete with others successfully, and manipulate them when necessary.

"Manipulation" has a negative connotation. It implies dishonesty. But while the dictionary gives the synonyms "juggle" and "falsify" it also defines it as the ability to "manage or influence by artful skill." Women who in general have greater interpersonal skills than men could be very good business and career manipulators if they were not afraid of this negative implication. Those who skillfully get others to do their bidding may attract resentment. Those women who are brought up to please find it very difficult to be the target of the anger of the person whom they have successfully outmaneuvered.

There are two aspects to liking someone which can be called *affection* and *respect*. A man can like a woman because of the way she relates to him personally, if she is kind and beautiful (affection) and experiences a feeling of emotional warmth and closeness toward her, or he can like her because of her abilities outside of their personal relations (respect). In a study of small groups by Robert Freed Bales at Harvard, the person with the best ideas, who contributes to problem solving, is rarely the best liked. The idea person dominates and gives directions and therefore frequently arouses hostility, while the one who smooths over disagreements receives affection. Traditionally women have been brought up to do the latter, to bring people together as hostess and make them feel good. Performing this role she is pleasing and thus liked. But when women try to lead, to be executives and get things done, to achieve respect rather than be liked, they may become very uncomfortable because of the hostility they may attract. The best leaders, of course, receive both respect and affection, the combined aspects of liking. Many women need to work on achieving respect because of their traditional upbringing, which prepares them to please in order to win affection. In the past, few women have gotten enough support from their fathers to develop into secure, competent adults. Rigid sex typing and the negative definition of feminine behavior have hurt them in their career efforts. Sex roles are becoming more flexible and women are developing a more positive self-concept with a wider range of competencies, and this will lead to more success in their careers.

Assertiveness training for women, which has enjoyed a recent vogue, is directly linked to the need for respect and the willingness to risk affection. To assert means to state with assurance, confidence, and force, something women brought up to seek affection and attempt to please find hard to do. Women are joining groups to learn what their fathers too often did not teach: the willingness to stand up for what they believe in the face of possible hostility. In order to make the most of her talents a woman must win respect. It is not enough in a career to be regarded with affection.

Along with the ego strength necessary to deal with the outer work world, a woman also must manage her inner needs and emotions. One of these is her affections, which are a strong part of her natural makeup. In the old days when a woman was usually just a secretary, if she fell in love with her boss she left her job and married him. Now if she is an executive and falls in love with an attractive male above, equal to, or below her in the hierarchy, she faces a much bigger problem because she does not want to abandon her serious career lightly. Consequently, controlling her sexual impulses at work is essential. To do so most effectively it is best if she is sure enough of herself to be warm and accepting without being flirtatious, rather than overly rejecting and cold. Being tense and unfriendly in order to guard against sexual expression is not a satisfactory solution. Not only must a woman control her own sexual expression toward attractive male colleagues she genuinely likes and admires, she must manage approaches made toward her. This must be done as gracefully as possible so as not to excessively jeopardize the ongoing work relationship.

Anger is another strong, potentially disruptive emotion that must be maturely managed. Differences among those with whom one works are inevitable and must be settled without violence or lasting scars. Anger should never be expressed thoughtlessly just for venting it. It may give temporary cathartic relief, but the damage done to work relationships can be permanent and irrevocable. The immediate pleasure of emotional discharge must be passed up in favor of long-term considerations. That is not to say that anger should never be expressed, but that much thought should be given to the consequences. Giving voice to hostility at the correct time can affect those toward whom it is directed and thus benefit a woman at the same time that tension is reduced.

A woman whose father has helped her grow to a healthy maturity is capable of being a self-starter. She does not look to bosses for orders, or use them as teachers to make sure she completes a task, but patiently perseveres until the job is finished. She is able to complete a project even in the face of opposition and setbacks. She makes the necessary decisions and stands by them, rather than considering endless alternatives and doing nothing.

Being a competent adult with respect to a career, possessing all the ego skills required to manage her outside and inside world, is something for which most fathers have not prepared their daughters in the past. While more seem to be doing so now, there is a large group of women who need to learn new career skills never taught at home. It is hard for them but certainly not impossible. Witness the greatly increased competence and position of women in business. But there is a lot of strain on them because they are trying to comfortably fill a role for which they have been inadequately prepared by their fathers.

WOMEN IN THE ORGANIZATION—FROM FATHER TO BOSS

To successfully climb the ladder of a business organization from entry level to executive a woman must make use of the skills and avoid the errors learned in her youth. In the corporation she must once again develop from dependent trainee to independent executive much as she did from child to self-reliant adult separate from her father. In fact, her career climb takes from age twenty-five to forty-five (twenty years), just the period of growth she had with her father. Her rise up the corporate ladder recapitulates her development into adulthood.

It is my hope that viewing your progress in an organization in this structured way will help you understand and maximize your strengths while overcoming your weaknesses. Once less anxious and myopic, you will feel less troubled about your career and more able to evaluate your work behavior and effectively change what troubles you.

Transference in Jobs is Very Common

In spite of some increase in the numbers of female executives most bosses are still men. When a woman enters an organization her superior will very likely be an older man, perhaps her father's age.

Freud's term transference or Harry Stack Sullivan's parataxic distortion refers to the misperceptions of others that we all unconsciously make. Looking at someone we see from two aspects: what is actually before us and what our experience and memory tells us it means. We judge whether the person is someone we would like to know. His or her accent and dress may be associated in our memory with someone we loved or feared. All these reactions happen rapidly and automatically. We judge very fast whom we like and dislike, whom at a cocktail party we want to talk to, who looks interesting, who is to be feared and avoided, who makes us uncomfortable. Some of our judgments are realistic and these are not transferences or parataxic distortions but based on the evidence before our eyes. Thus two people can agree that so-and-so is a boss to be feared. But many of our reactions take place rapidly, automatically, and completely outside of our consciousness. The more a woman knows about how she related to her father, what support she expected and what harm she feared, the more she will be able to recognize the same reactions toward her male or female superiors in the organization and the better able she will be to control and correct her distortions. It is not that the older man behind the desk reminds her of her father because he looks like him, but that her expectations and attitudes are automatically colored by the inequality in the power between them.

Before getting into some of the specific forms transference can take, the fundamental, summary one is the feeling that you are basically acceptable or unacceptable, and you can do something to influence this. Most of us have been brought up to feel we are basically acceptable to others with more or less emphasis having been placed on how hard we have to work to achieve this. While we all desire total acceptance without effort, it is to our advantage, at least in the work world, to be used to having to earn it. "Only God . . . could love you for yourself alone and not your yellow hair," Yeats wrote.

If people do not feel accepted no matter what they do, they suffer basic insecurity and chronic discomforting anxiety. Such people find it very hard to work in an organization and if they do their distress prevents them from progressing very far. But for the great majority who have had the experience in childhood of being acceptable to their fathers—indeed loved —they are able to emotionally expect and accept good feelings in relation to their bosses. These are certainly not present all the time, but the basic underlying security is there to get them over the rough spots.

Transference is so subtle and automatic that most women are unaware of its effect on their corporate climb. For example, if a daughter was adored and encouraged by her father, she expects the same from her boss. Doing a good job, turning a good phrase in a letter or report, she expects her superior to be delighted, and when all he does is point out her spelling error or suggest that she add or delete a sentence she is outraged. Her emotional set is an expectation of praise. Aware of her fury at her ungrateful boss, she is not conscious of the source of her childish outrage. Senior male executives are not delighted with turns of phrase in the way fathers are about the bright sayings of their little four-year-old daughters.

The unnoticed expectation of constant reinforcement and encouragement is another childhood vestige that can deter a woman's corporate climb. So much a part of her that she does not realize it is excessive, she either demands too much of her boss, leading to his annoyance and her disappointment in him, or she pretends self-sufficiency while experiencing almost constant terror.

If the adored and coddled daughter has problems relating to her male superiors, then the criticized, ignored, or mistreated one has even more. She avoids her boss out of fear and overreacts to his criticism. Never having felt basically acceptable to her father, she gets too upset whenever she displeases an authority. Paradoxically, because she has the long-standing emotional habit of feeling her father's displeasure, she seems to attract more than her share from the boss. Her transference comes true as she unconsciously re-creates the scene of her early life in the office. The boss becomes just like her father and criticizes her.

The argumentative young woman on the job is often one stuck at the level of adolescent battle with her father. She needs to emotionally engage with authority, while at the same time trying to do without it. Such a woman might go in and ask her boss how she should do a task and then argue with him that his suggestion is wrong. Not independent enough to proceed on her own, she is not childish enough to follow orders.

There are two types of male superiors a woman becomes involved with in the organization—those she picks and those she is assigned. Over the former she has control and transference plays an even more powerful role. Who her father is and how she has related to him over the span of her life strongly influences whom she goes to work for and how she will thereafter relate to him. Not too different from picking a husband, she selects someone just like dad, or his opposite, or if she understands herself fairly well she chooses her male superior rationally from the standpoint of the development of her career.

Barbara Casey has had eleven jobs in thirteen years and feels hopeless about ever finding satisfaction in her work or being able to advance. The trouble is the men she selects to work for and how she relates to them. On the surface she is a daddy's girl, able to charm and please older men quickly in interviews and to feel the hope that this time it will be different. If only she could continue to feel close to the man for whom she has chosen to work she could remain in one place while she climbed the corporate ladder. But she always becomes disappointed in him, quits, and is unemployed for a while because she feels hopeless about overcoming her repetitious problem. The main reason she has not solved her difficulty is her failure to see it as a transference pattern. Instead she experiences it as a series of single, different failures: one boss was too demanding, another mentally disturbed, a third an inadequate leader, a fourth sexually demanding, a fifth too self-important, and on and on.

Barbara's father is a surgeon who expected his daughters to hop like operating-room nurses. She could not stand this about him yet longed for him to order her about. She was drawn to his attractive, brilliant capabilities while terrified of his fierce authoritarian impatience and intolerance of disobedience. Each boss brought new hope of close collaboration dashed by fear of and rebellion against those who were powerful like father and contempt for those who were softer. Unconsciously picking men just like or totally unlike her male parent, she blindly reenacted the unhappy pattern. Finally she sought psychiatric aid and slowly overcame her male authority problem.

Most of the psychiatric work with Barbara centered on the first thirty seconds spent with a prospective new boss. She analyzed her perceptions of him with a view toward eliminating the distortions. If an able male authority frightened her and an inept one made her contemptuous, no work relationship would ever be successful. Because a boss knew what he wanted and told her so in an initial interview was no reason to feel excitedly attracted to him like a little girl, completely afraid of his harsh criticism should she make a mistake, and adolescently rebellious in her growing desire to tell him off and leave. She realized that she liked bosses who knew what they wanted from her and that not all of them would crush her as her arrogant father did when she made a mistake. The ability to see the difference between a cruel tyrant and a benevolent despot made all the difference. Before, as soon as she had seen a strong definite male she had made automatic transference assumptions and expectations, all of which became self-fulfilling prophecies. Now she could see reality in the light of the present, undistorted by experiences from the past.

BEING HIRED—THE CHILDLIKE OASIS REVISITED

Being hired is a vote of confidence, an act of acceptance. You are given the job because you are liked, thought attractive, and believed to be competent. Once there, you are anxious to please and make a good impression. A young woman recently hired is in a position very similar to her childhood oasis, in which she is liked and has little or no responsibility. She is expected to make mistakes and is forgiven because she is young and inexperienced. She is a student who needs to learn and when she gets a salary raise it is like a good report card. Her central concern is to prove herself in traditional elementary school terms. Conduct is important and she behaves shyly in her desire to be liked and to show her willingness to learn. Like a child she takes criticism very personally. She feels timid and afraid.

The beginning young woman employee serves initially as merely an extension of her boss. She types the letter rather than offer her opinion of it. In time she or her boss, alone or together, as part of a natural occurrence or arbitrarily, will recognize that she needs and deserves more independence and that she is ready for it.

PROBLEMS OF THE CHILDLIKE OR
ENTRY-LEVEL POSITION

The level of development that a young woman has achieved at the time she is hired strongly influences the kinds of problems she will have. An immature oasis girl might find herself settled into a lifetime position, glad to be appreciated and told what to do, to feel no demands and to be secure. Her father-boss will deal with the harsh world for her, while she pleases him and makes him happy. Other oasis-stuck girls may have been so spoiled by doting fathers as to be unable to continue working at all. Bosses' reasonable requests are expe-

rienced as harsh demands and these women angrily quit job
after job.

The adolescent-level girl has problems with the realistic
need to employ childlike techniques in her entry-level position. She does not like following her boss's orders cheerfully
and without argument. She feels confined by the organization's rules and demands and becomes *angry*. Desiring to
express her own creativity, believing she knows better than
her elders, she feels above it all and that the job does not
fulfill her needs, desires, and talents. Adolescent-level women
are self-centered and have trouble recognizing and meeting
the needs of others in the organization. In addition they may
not be very dependable or punctual. As women become better educated their expectations for job fulfillment rise and
those who remain immature have no patience for working
their way up in an organization, especially from entry-level
positions which are fairly mindless.

Adult women recognize they have to learn the trade and
pay their dues. They accept the need to regress to a childlike
entry-level position, tolerating boredom, the humiliation of
being told what to do sometimes by someone not as intelligent, while remaining pleasant and cooperative. While realizing the need for a good working relationship with their boss,
they will be less dependent upon his complete acceptance and
will start to build a network of friends throughout the organization. She recognizes that she will not be typing letters forever and is aware of the need to learn what every piece of
paper that crosses her desk means. She is curious, anxious to
learn, completely dependable, and competent in her job. Usually she finds a place within the entry-level position where she
can demonstrate her creativity and competence. Once she is
recognized she is promoted to a mid-level job where she will
function on an adolescent corporate level.

MIDDLE MANAGEMENT—THE ADOLESCENT
CORPORATE LEVEL AND ITS PROBLEMS

The adolescent woman who is too impatient, self-centered, rebellious, and angry will not be promoted to middle management at all but will fail to survive her entry-level position. The more controlled adolescent woman will become a middle manager, but she will not advance further unless she matures more. Her teenage ways will keep her from top-level posts.

The adolescent-stuck woman will not advance further for the following reasons. Her mixture of independence and dependence is accentuated by her promotion to middle-management rank. She still needs and has a boss (father) but resents him. Like a fifteen-year-old she unconsciously invites his intrusion by her behavior, which she then angrily rejects. She seeks attention, sometimes immaturely, but will not admit it to herself.

Most authorities agree that women are more emotional in business than men. But certainly the adolescent-like ones lack enough control of their tears, fears, frustrations, and rage. This upsets the male-dominated upper echelons and blocks their advancement.

Because the adolescently immature woman retains her teenage self-centeredness she lacks organizational perspective and is unable to and uninterested in assessing the needs of others. Those below her suffer from her inability to be sensitive to their concerns and to adequately motivate and reward them. Those above feel her dependence and anger, but notice her lack of sympathy and empathy for their problems. Instead of showing genuine interest in others throughout the organization and building a network, she alienates them with her selfish ambition.

Her boss finds such an adolescent woman hard to work with and feels little inclined to promote her. Instead of a collaborative spirit, an ally on whom he can rely and in whom he can confide, her superior finds an angry, moody, touchy subordinate who takes things too personally and fails to realize that he also has problems bigger than she. She believes the sun rises and sets on her. Her immaturity also makes her impatient for immediate gratification in salary raises and promotions. Yet if she gets them she becomes frightened by the responsibility.

Adolescent-like adult women in organizations have trouble managing others. When something goes wrong they may become too angry or upset. Their sense of self does not provide proper defenses to insulate them from the daily problems and pressures of managing personnel. Saying no to the requests of those who work for them is difficult. Wishing to be liked, the adolescent female manager is too nice. She imagines the reaction of underlings to a denied request to be rage like hers when her wishes are blocked. Finally, because she is self-centered and wants all credit for herself, she does not openly recognize the good work of those in her employ. This demoralizes those beneath her to the detriment of the organization.

Sex is a problem for all women in the male corporate world, but especially for the adolescent-like one who is awakened erotically but not sure of the proper time and place. She is tempted to use sex as a shortcut to get ahead, especially since she lacks the adult skills required to achieve through proper channels. But she is ambivalent and is repulsed by the thought of using her body for advancement. She knows it is a dangerous and inadequate method for success, that it can result in her being exploited and then fired. Some adult women with teenage minds are not so coolly calculating about using sex, but genuinely fall in love with their male bosses and, having poor impulse control, give in to their carnal desires. The result is usually a mess.

There are also wonderful sides to adolescents that must be remembered. Middle managers of this type can overflow with ideas and energy, producing innovations and daring to try methods more cautious adultlike leaders would not. The charm of their idealism and new perspectives can fire those below them with the desire to attempt what they otherwise would not dare.

THE OASIS GIRL AND THE ADULT WOMAN IN MIDDLE MANAGEMENT

The oasis girl occasionally gets promoted to middle management as a reward for years of faithful service. Usually it is a disaster for her unless she is able to grow into the new status. She is very frightened of responsibility and keeps running to those above her for reassurance and direction. If they are patient with her, take a lot of time, and give much support, she may be able to make the transition and learn to do more for herself. But if she remains a little girl she will exhaust them with her fearful dependence and irritate them with her childish need to blame everyone but herself when something goes wrong.

The adult woman does not have so many problems as a middle manager, except to be patient in her wait for advancement to senior level and to suffer her superior, especially if he is her intellectual and managerial inferior. But being grown up means managing such feelings, not being too angry, and empathizing with your boss rather than competing with him. She recognizes that her success is connected to his and that conflict with him is not worth it. She does not take things too personally, which limits her emotional reactions to their interactions. She is able to ask him for what she really needs and to do so in a comfortable way. She sees him as he really is with the clarity with which the adult woman is able to assess her father's strengths and to forgive him his weaknesses. She relates to him as a free-standing mature colleague, no longer as a dependent or angry child. If something goes wrong she accepts responsibility.

She has gone through all three stages. Having started in the organization as a child she has learned from her teachers, attended to details, and gradually increased her responsibilities starting from the most menial. As an adolescent in the organization she has become more of an individual and knowledgeable. She has handled the period between childhood and adulthood in such a way as to show herself an increasingly responsible individual who is worthy and capable of making the organization like and respect her. Now able to accept full responsibility, not too dependent on the support of superiors, not too deeply angry, she is ready to be a boss-parent herself, a member of senior management.

THE ADULT WOMAN

Lauren Doyle has made it to the top of a large movie studio. Her considerable talents—both as a director and producer in the creative area and as a businessperson with marketing experience—has brought her to the top of a mainly male-dominated field. Her tenacity and talent have been rewarded. She has developed powerful friends high up in her organization who

have promoted and who protect her against others who are
jealous and would like to see her stall or be fired. In the past
she made the mistake of sleeping with her benefactors, but
now she is able to keep her business relationships on a professional basis. But she is wise enough to make sure they thrive
and continue, knowing well that otherwise her enemies might
get her.

She has learned how to behave. Although she likes to direct
films herself, she knows that as a female executive she had
better stay in the corporate suite and let others do it. She has
regrets about the loss of this creative expression but she understands the necessity of presenting the proper façade to the
organization in order to reach her goal as an executive.

She has gotten to where she is partly because of and partly
in spite of her father, plus more than five years of psychoanalysis. Her father, an automotive executive, served as an example for her, although he was largely absent during her form-
ative years. He has taken little interest in her career and
does not realize how far she has risen. When a famous friend
of his lost his secretary he suggested that she take the job. Because she is mature she did not scream at her father, but
sadly recognized his failure to understand how much more
than a secretary she had become. She also forgave him his
frequent questions about what short films she was making
and his unwillingness to comprehend that she had risen so
high in the corporate structure that producing films was beneath her. She now made sure that others made films and was
involved with overall corporate planning.

Lauren has made many mistakes on the job that she would
not have made if her father had been a better model. Since
many women have not had male parents take their careers
seriously, Lauren is an example of how experience, determi-

nation, and psychotherapy can overcome problems in the corporate climb.

THE ADULT WOMAN'S RISE

Once a woman realizes realistically, rather than as a confused adolescent, that her boss is no more capable than she, knows no more, and cannot see the future any better but has just been there longer, she is ready for senior management. She thinks she would be valuable in a top role because she has the experience and knows more than others in the organization. She has given up her dependent status and has a sense of her competence and individuality. She is willing to take risks without requiring constant support and to accept the consequences should she fail. She can comfortably withstand the loneliness of decision making at the top. She realizes the importance of action and of avoiding the paralysis of fear. She makes ten decisions a day with the knowledge that three will be good, three bad and four mediocre. No one can be a senior executive without the willingness to risk being wrong.

The adult woman executive has completed her second cycle of maturation. The first was in relation to her father as she advanced from his adored little girl to an adolescent shifting back and forth between dependence and independence to an adult who is separate but equal. Similarly in her career she began as a child full of promise, needing direction and training, grew to an adolescent capable of some responsibility but requiring limits and guidance, and finally became a mature person capable of leadership.

Four

INSECURITY

You are an insecure person if you feel excessively afraid, unsafe, unprotected, unable to cope with or control yourself or your environment. Everyone feels unsure under conditions which threaten psychological or physical safety or at times when memories of childhood helplessness are evoked. Whenever people are confronted with a new or dangerous situation, insecure feelings come back. For example, almost everyone uses alcohol to calm fears of appearing unacceptable, foolish, or uninteresting to others at a cocktail party. Similarly, the ancient Greeks drank wine at Symposia to loosen inhibitions, because it was more effective than food in getting each of the guests to risk taking a turn at entertaining the assembled. While everyone is disturbed under perilous conditions not everyone can be called an insecure person. We refer to someone as insecure when he or she cannot function because of fear or experiences anxiety at a time when a confident person would not. How insecure a woman feels is directly related to the amount of anxiety she experiences and to the status of her self-esteem.

If security is safety then anxiety is the opposite. The more anxious you are for whatever underlying reasons the greater your expectation that your efforts will be unsuccessful. Those who do not expect their attempts to succeed are insecure. If you don't think men will like you or find you attractive, you will not confidently look forward to meeting them. If you experience undue fear when being judged you will expect to make a poor impression in a job interview. The more anxiety a woman has, the less capable she feels when dealing with people and situations.

Insecurity is so uncomfortable that people become experts in avoiding it. The methods they use quickly become automatic parts of their personalities, which often function outside of awareness and can severely limit their freedom to grow. An insecure woman may remain a little girl at work or with men, thus avoiding adult challenge by remaining the child of her boss or lover. Or she may function as a competent executive routinely, but become too dependent and overwhelmed in an unusual or pressure-packed situation.

According to Harry Stack Sullivan, self-esteem is directly related both to the amount of anxiety an individual experiences in daily life and to the capacity she possesses to deal with it effectively. Thus, self-esteem is weakened by anxiety and insecurity. While everyone lacks confidence at times, we do not all suffer from low self-regard. Self-esteem or its lack is the reputation a woman acquires with herself. High regard for herself enables a woman to overcome her insecurities. For example, a young woman in college may be frightened by mathematics, having been encouraged as a child not to bother her pretty head about such things. Her level of self-esteem allows her to approach her mathematical insecurity in one of two ways. If low, she will avoid it and all related fields for the rest of her life, but if high she may attempt to overcome this sex-related handicap. She may angrily decide to show her parents and anyone else who believes her to be a math failure that she can conquer it. Self-esteem is required to cope with the realistic feelings of helplessness and powerlessness inevitably arising in an individual's lifetime.

Self-esteem is made up of two parts: self-confidence (competence) and self-respect (a feeling one is worthy or worthwhile). Self-esteem is not a conscious, verbalized judgment but a constantly experienced automatic part of every other feeling. It is the conviction that one is competent to judge, think, and correct one's errors.

FOUR KINDS OF INSECURITY: RECOGNIZED, UNRECOGNIZED, JUSTIFIED, AND IMMATURE

There are four kinds of insecurity. The first is *recognized*, in which a woman is aware of being uncertain about her ability to act effectively in one or more situations. People tend to keep away from circumstances in which they feel ineffective because of the discomfort they experience in them. If a woman is uneasy about the judgment of strangers and consequently avoids interviews, she narrows her horizons by remaining home or in a job she has otherwise outgrown. Such habitual avoidances of fear can lead to a very common second type of insecurity, the *unrecognized*. Here the avoidance is so automatic a woman is no longer aware of limiting herself because of apprehension. It becomes part of her character. A woman who was once brighter and better educated than her husband now becomes flustered and unable to talk about serious subjects requiring thought. She tells stories and keeps the conversation going at the family dinner table but she does not understand finance, politics, or her husband's business. As long as she plays her role of housewife and mother she feels secure, and is in fact unaware of her self-imposed limitations.

A third type of insecurity is *justified* because there is good reason for it. Those who attempt a task for which they are improperly trained and prepared feel anxious with good reason. Such fear can serve as a signal to do one's homework. Where some oasis girls get in trouble is by attempts to use charm to avoid the unpleasantness of facing and conquering justified insecurities.

The last kind of insecurity results from failure to complete the stages of development and is therefore *immature*. Whenever a woman finds herself in a situation requiring performance above her developmental level she feels uncertain. When an oasis girl, for example, is placed in a role of leadership, whether in the home or on the job, she becomes upset, confused, depressed, frightened, or angry as her previously held dependent security vanishes. It is the unproductive defense mechanisms and behaviors from the past that contribute to insecurities in all of us because they interfere with the forging of new skills required to effectively deal with the present. Those who avoid adult challenge or live in a world of fantasy cannot, indeed will not, cope with the demanding and interesting problems arising in their work and in their personal lives.

Insecurities color every corner of our lives. Those who avoid them totally never grow, develop, and change with the passage of time. They are unable to adapt. If you are unwilling or unprepared to bear the normal insecurity that accompanies risk taking you may end up vegetating in the same job or in a dull and lifeless relationship in which you hold on to your partner out of fear or habit.

Since we all have insecurities and since they may become such automatic and habitual parts of our personalities that we barely notice the full extent of them, it is helpful to think of them in stages as a way of understanding and effectively overcoming them.

While fathers are not the only source of a woman's security and ability to cope with the complexities of adult life, they exert an important and major effect. The best way for you to understand your recognized and unrecognized insecurities, to cope with your justified and overcome your immature ones, is to perceive the level of development you have reached and how it was and is affected by your relationship to your father.

STAGES IN THE DEVELOPMENT OF SELF-ESTEEM

Self-esteem represents the individual's global positive or negative attitude toward himself or herself and provides the energy by which insecurities are met and overcome. In adults it is based on a realistic assessment of intelligence, honesty, diligence, and good behavior. Grown women who base their self-appraisal excessively on fantasy or who avoid the justified insecurity caused by facing new and difficult tasks are unable to address their lives realistically and effectively and their feelings of self-worth rest on a shaky base, since they cannot fool themselves all the time. When positive self-regard depends on daydreams, lies, and avoidance, the discrepancy between fantasy and reality soon becomes apparent. Calling yourself a pianist when you last practiced regularly or gave a concert ten years ago fools no one, not even yourself.

Self-esteem in the Oasis Period

Young children tend to inflate their self-qualities. The three-year-old girl puts on her tutu and dances *Swan Lake* in the living room to the delight of her parents, who tell her it was wonderful. A child must not be judged by adult standards of performance and needs to be encouraged. When she draws a picture, plays the piano, or appears in a new dress she is told how wonderful and pretty she is. Objective tests of children have shown they consistently overrate the prestige of their racial and ethnic group and the status of their father's occupation. The oasis period is necessarily, therefore, a time of love, and acceptance to encourage the developing young girl to try new and difficult tasks and to provide a place to come for recovery and comfort should she fail. Her self-esteem needs to be inflated unrealistically in order to give this little person the courage and confidence to try things in the big, scary world. If children saw themselves as they really are —small, vulnerable, uneducated, not able to cope, not special but average—they would feel defeated, depressed, and unwilling to attempt the previously untried. It would be bad for our world if the "unrealistic" hopes and expectations of young people did not give them the spark to try the new things that will advance our civilization.

The oasis girl should feel secure with her daddy in a romantic, unchallenging world in which she is the center of his attention and the recipient of his undemanding love. It forms a necessary base for her future and yet the possibilities for problems are very great. It is easy for fathers to err and provide too much or too little during the oasis period. Too little results when fathers are too busy, do not like their little girls, or are uncomfortable with them. Women deprived of father's love and attention in childhood have underdeveloped self-esteem and find it hard to believe a man could totally love and accept them. Too much support and attention results when fathers are otherwise unhappy in their work or with their wives and turn to their little girls as a primary or only source of happiness. In such instances the unrealistic total acceptance of childhood remains dominant through adult life and results in women who expect to be totally accepted, loved, admired, and the center of attention wherever they go.

When a grown woman's self-esteem retains too much of the oasis period, she is too dependent on others to protect her and admire her efforts. Because her fragile self-regard is built on an unrealistic, childlike base, she becomes excessively anxious and upset should her own or someone else's opinion of her be diminished. This total dependence on outside sources for self-esteem makes her unable to absorb minor criticisms and frustrations. She has great difficulty in a job where her boss is not a comfortable, supportive figure, but demands that she be mature and self-sufficient. When he does not completely protect her and admire her efforts and when she is not the center of his attention she cannot function happily. Similar problems occur with boyfriends and often such women look to older men to give them either what they never had in childhood or what they had too much of. Socially such a woman must either be the center of attention or attach herself to a superstar (lover, friend, teacher, parent) so this other person will provide her with an emotional high and allow her to base her self-esteem on fantasy.

Oasis-stuck girls find it very difficult to test themselves in the real, adult world. Because they are not used to realistically confronting their own strengths and weaknesses and facing their limitations and instead have an exaggerated—albeit untested—sense of self-worth and importance, their real skills tend to be undeveloped and their willingness and capacity to cope with stress and possible failure untried. They are likely to feel panicked and overwhelmed when confronted with difficult, complex adult problems.

Self-esteem in Adolescence

As a little girl grows up and enters adolescence she is no longer the oasis child whose every effort is praised and encouraged, but a young woman of whom more is expected. She is judged more exactingly by parents and teachers as well as by her peers, who are sometimes harsh. More separate from her father and mother, she becomes more involved with girls her own age who provide her with both support and criticism. She becomes attached to a best friend to whom she tells all her secrets and with whom she spends long hours on the phone. Father and mother are thus replaced, at least in part. She becomes influenced by how her friends dress and behave and very much needs their approval. She is a Person in a Pack supported by a best friend.

The move from parents to the bigger world, occurring around the age of twelve, is associated with a sharp fall in self-esteem. The drop is painful and accompanied by all the symptoms of this threat to the feeling of well-being. Girls this age feel anxious, irritable, angry, and depressed and are usually unaware that the underlying reason is low self-esteem. They try to limit their anxiety by clinging to their best friend and by conforming to the peer group they admire and to whom they look for support. Fathers and mothers are alternately viewed as comforts and as enemies restricting their freedom.

An ingenious study of 1917 pupils in twenty-five Baltimore City public schools between grades three and twelve was reported in the *American Sociological Review* in 1973. Using both a global measure and a specific of self-esteem (e.g., being smart, good-looking, truthful, good at sports, well-behaved, hardworking in school, helpful, humorous), the investigators were able to document a sharp decline in self-esteem among twelve-year-olds, especially those in junior high school rather than in the sixth grade of elementary school. This negative self-attitude continued into late adolescence. That this feeling persists into the seventeen-to-nineteen-year age range is confirmed by other studies of college students which find low self-esteem the norm rather than the exception. The dean of freshmen at Harvard understands this when he greets the entering class by saying, "Each of you is convinced he or she got in here by accident."

There are a number of reasons for this downturn in self-esteem at age twelve. The main one is the loss of father's (and mother's) unconditional love and acceptance, replaced by the more exacting judgments of teachers and peers. No longer her father's brilliant, beautiful little girl, the daughter receives objective grades on tests and has to compete for the attention of boys. No matter how successful she is at both, the doubt and anxiety over achievement is very different from the warm, undemanding certainty of the oasis. That twelve-year-olds have higher self-esteem when in the sixth grade of elementary school than those the same age who are in junior high school illustrates the importance of the environment on self-esteem at this age. Elementary schools are more like an oasis for the oldest children in them, while in junior high school they are the youngest, are not used to having a teacher for each subject, and are in a bigger, impersonal institution.

Bodily and hormonal changes also threaten self-esteem, as the girl feels less in control of her physical and emotional being. She does not quite know how to behave. Self-confidence is the conviction that one is competent to think, to judge, to know and to correct one's errors. The girl is physically mature but unsure of how to function in adult social roles.

Adolescent self-esteem is based more on people than on facts. People, not reason, constitute the major tool of survival. Reality becomes reality as judged by others. The adolescent must understand, please, deceive, maneuver, manipulate, or obey them. Because she is not yet focused enough on objective reality she must grasp and satisfy the expectations, conditions, and values of those around her. The temporary diminution of anxiety resulting from winning the approval of others is her substitute for self-esteem. In her mind other people's judgments occupy the place which for a mature person is occupied by reality. In order to belong *with* others she is willing to belong *to* them. She lives under blackmail in her insecurity.

For the adolescent girl her father still plays an important role. If he becomes frightened of her woman's body and withdraws or if he is too interested in it she will feel less comfortable about herself and with boys. Fathers at this time are most often in their forties and facing their own adolescent-like concerns about career, sex, and identity, although without their daughters' limitless view of time. A father who remains appropriately close to his teenage daughter may enjoy the talks, ideas, poetry, and physical beauty of adolescence while suffering the rebellion, moodiness, fights, and selfishness. A girl lucky enough to have an involved father during this stormy yet lovely time is much benefited by his authoritative guidance in learning how to deal with men and in the development of her own self-esteem. As he copes with and negotiates the tricky shoals of adolescence with her she learns from him. The incorporation of his strengths builds up her own. She learns to be confident about her ability to conquer com-

plicated and difficult new situations by watching and learning
as he interacts with her.

For the woman who never progresses beyond adolescent-
level self-esteem a lifelong excessive dependence on the approval of the group results. She will always live according to
the rules set by others and lack the courage to take responsibility. By holding the minds of other persons rather than objective reality as her ultimate frame of reference she remains
a follower, not a leader, unable to make independent judgments or think on her own. The careers of such women will
not include promotion to senior management unless they
change. They are also unlikely to make very good marriages,
since they will either be too dependent on their husbands or
too ready to rebel as a counterreaction. These women will
idealize or deprecate those they love or for whom they work
as the need to look up to or rebel against their dependence on
them fluctuates. A woman who fails to develop mature self-
esteem based on effective coping with the realities of her life
is destined to remain moody and mercurial as she experiences
the hope of comfort and salvation from new people followed
by rapid disappointment when they fail her. Often using sex
as a prop for her fragile self-esteem, she becomes depressed
or enraged when her new man is, like all the others, unable to
rescue her from the rollercoaster ups and downs of her life.
Because these women are too dependent on others they do
not possess a gyroscope in the form of an internal feeling of
self-esteem which serves to regulate their emotional life
against the inevitable frustrations and disappointments we all
encounter.

Lifelong dependence on approval of the group can also
lead to what Matina Horner described as the "avoidance of
success" arising from the fear of appearing unfeminine or
being socially rejected. Historically women have been less

willing than men to risk being disliked while scrambling up the corporate ladder. Given the choice between being competent or being lovable they have chosen the latter.

Presently more and more women wish to be successful in their chosen careers, but too often find themselves hampered by immature self-esteem. Their previously held dependent security vanishes once they are called upon to make decisions and exert leadership. Two such immature women vacillating between childhood and adolescent self-esteem illustrate the problem.

Two Women with Immature Self-esteem

Barbara Wright is in her early twenties. She tries very hard, but finds that women and men her own age disappoint her. Her peers always seemed selfish compared to her parents. They had her when they were quite old (mother forty and father forty-five) and she is their only child. Naturally they doted on her. Girlfriends and especially boyfriends never treated her nearly so well. Barbara is charming and delightful to older men. She is very bright and definitely her father's daughter. A self-made millionaire, he would like her to be masterful enough to take over his business but insecure enough to need him. Her mother is the much weaker parent, one who is sad, incompetent, and unfulfilled. Barbara's conflict between the competence and incompetence within her was sapping her strength. Having achieved a perfect board score of 800, she is now in danger of flunking out of school. She interviews for jobs but is not hired. Her unrecognized attachment to her father keeps her from using her considerable natural talent to break away from him and become independent. The only time she is happy is when she's joking around with acquaintances. Whenever relations with her peers become serious or competitive she ends up feeling jealous, inferior, or hurt.

She will not participate in classes, believing those that do are willing to say the obvious in order to impress the teacher. Her silence enables her to feel superior to her classmates and has its origin in her childlike self-esteem in which she brilliantly stood and still stands above everyone, united with her daddy. They know better and are more successful than everyone else. Unfortunately, the adolescent part of her self-esteem is not so satisfied and sees her as not creative, slow-witted, and unable to get jokes quickly. She feels inferior to her classmates, less aggressive, unable to think as clearly, and much less likely to be offered a good job after graduation.

This brilliant young woman feels secure and superior like a child attached to her father and insecure like an adolescent whenever she attempts to succeed independently or be close to a man of her own. In fact, what made her withdraw even more into her oasis was rejection by a young man for whom she cared. Her perfect board scores, showing unlimited childlike potential, were enough for her. Mixing it up in the world involves the risk of insecurity and pain. Her father made the oasis too warm, secure, and attractive for her to be willing to do much venturing out. As soon as she was hurt she rushed back into the oasis to stay. Someone will have to help her get away from her lonely, brilliant, grasping father.

The second woman, Joan King, is even brighter than the first. Daughter of a world-renowned, socially inept near-genius, she delighted him from early childhood by her ability to learn complicated adult material and to compete well in their chess games. Joan's oasis was spent at the top of her class and high in his regard.

When she reached age twelve her father became busier and busier as his fame spread. She continued brilliantly in school, but he no longer noticed. She was never accepted socially by her adolescent classmates and felt unfeminine, a "joke" compared to her popular brothers and sisters. Her peer-dependent adolescent-like self-esteem remained very low and caused her great pain. She gained weight, felt unacceptable, and withdrew into her work. But even this suffered when the few boys and girls she allowed close disappointed her. Lacking the necessary support an adolescent girl still needs from an interested and helpful father, she was unable to withstand the inevitable teenage hurts and rejections and based more and more of her self-esteem on her previously successful oasis level. She avoided intimacy and became a workaholic who prided herself on being able to solve problems creatively and brilliantly. Looking on the surface as though she were mature and successful, she in fact continued to suffer a great deal from loneliness and depression. Overweight, she felt deeply ashamed of her appearance and spent her few leisure hours alone. Her only solid comfort came from using the mind which once had delighted her father. But when neither he nor any other intimate noticed, the promotions and raises she received at work were not enough and gave her insufficient pleasure.

Like an adolescent she would initially overidealize a new boss in her lonely search for a fatherlike authority who cared and noticed. But before very long she would become angry at the seeming indifference and ineptitude of her immediate superior. Having placed so much emphasis on the oasislike perfection of her intelligence (which was truly excellent), she could not take the smallest criticism or suggestion without feeling inadequate and devoid of all personal worth. Lacking an adult's true independence of mind, which is able to consider criticism and take correction, she had the child's inflated self-esteem, had to know it all, and became extremely defensive whenever her grandiosity was threatened.

The Need for Maturity

Childlike and adolescent-level self-esteem can suffice when benevolent bosses and husbands look after such women all their lives. They can be secure and happy as they charm the people whose support they require. But immature women are at risk. Times change. Children grow up and move away. The modern female is no longer regarded as or wants to be a decoration, but works, contributes to the family economy, has interesting things to do and say. Loyal secretaries are not always honored as they once were. As their consciousness is raised, they may feel unhappy and dissatisfied getting coffee and dutifully typing letters. People want to fulfill their potential, to be intellectually alive.

More and more present-day fathers realize the need for their daughters to be equipped for the complexities of modern life, to be able to work, be independent, use their gifts fully, and be equals of men. Unfortunately there is a generation caught in the middle, brought up to be old-fashioned at a time when the childlike or adolescent woman is out of favor. These women must now adapt and mature or face angry disappointment and bewilderment over changing expectations. Having failed to do so in their twenties they may finally become adults in their thirties, forties, or even fifties. The process can be painful but the rewards great as they begin to feel competent and self-reliant.

Aristotle defined happiness as an activity of soul in accordance with virtue, by which he meant it was in the nature of humans to be most content when using their highest faculties in the pursuit of excellence. Men and women were not happiest lying on the beach, he believed, but when acting or using their minds in ways they could respect. Modern research confirmed Aristotle's view. A large Texas study of leisure time found that most people reported feeling most gratified and happy when engaged in active pursuits they respected and least when merely resting and relaxing.

Adult Security and Self-esteem

Otto Rank conceptualized three stages in the process of becoming a fully mature adult. The first stage described by this contemporary of Freud finds the adult able to will for him or herself that which had before been determined by parents and society. The average normal adult is fixed at this level and lives uncreatively but comfortably. Such people are *conformists*. They wear the right clothes at the country club, they follow rather than set the styles, and they make competent administrators of stable business organizations no longer growing. Their conformity is self-imposed rather than dictated by school, parents, or society and in this sense they are self-motivated adults rather than children or adolescents.

Rank's second stage we would nowadays call one of transition. Such individuals feel estranged from society, cannot accept its dictates, but do not have the strength to create their own values. Such people rebel against others, but are unable to think through and act on their own standards.

The third and highest stage of individuation (in today's jargon "being one's own person") is achieved when an individual is able to be creative and to act in accordance with his or her own ideals. Neither helplessly driven by a Freudian id nor restrained by a Freudian superego, such people function independently, governed by their beliefs, and are masters of themselves.

Rank's ideas of progressive adult levels, conceived long ago, remain modern in spirit as they coincide with our current research into the stages of adult development. Young adults, just having learned to stand apart from their parents, conform insecurely to what they think is right. Those destined to develop further first rebel against society's norms and then live in accordance with their own version of what is right. Rank's conception of the steps to adult maturity is similar to those I have described in women's careers, starting by conforming in an entry-level position, being more independent in middle management, and finally becoming a leader. As women struggle to separate from their fathers they initially conform or rebel before learning to stand on their own.

A fully realized adult woman does not depend on others for her self-esteem. In fact, she expects others to *perceive* her value, not to *create* it. She does not desire approval indiscriminately or for its own sake, but only if it is expressed because of attributes she respects in herself. She is not so much concerned with what someone thinks of her as with what *she* thinks of him or her. Unlike a child stuck with parents, family, or teachers, she picks her own intimates according to standards she creates.

Thus the question is raised of how open the fully realized adult is to criticism, opinions of others, fads, changing moralities, and behaviors. A perfect set of internal, tight values would make anyone smug and unbearable. No adult is completely self-sufficient and secure. Only the grandiose grown-up child tries to maintain such a stance. The creative adult has the strength to face her insecurities, bear the anxieties they cause, and patiently attempt to overcome them. This leads to a deeper sense of self-worth. Confronted by insecurity, the oasis child hides and won't try, the adolescent is horribly afraid and conforms, while the adult attempts to conquer.

Being adult and solid in self-esteem does not free a woman from all pain and insecurity. Whenever a person is rejected by a loved one, becomes seriously ill physically, or experiences a major work disappointment, earlier insecurity and self-esteem levels are activated. Our conscious and unconscious memories are long. Losing someone close automatically resonates the pain of absent loved ones. Failing to win a promotion or being fired drives self-esteem down and back to early-adolescent discomfort and childhood helplessness. The difference between the mature and immature person does not lie so much in terms of the degree of discomfort from anxiety and depression they experience as in their resilience. The ability to bounce back, to realize the setback does not reflect complete worthlessness, to mourn it, learn from it, and put it in perspective is how the mature woman copes with and overcomes major disappointments.

The adult woman accepts her need for help at times of trial. Not overly dependent on others for approval, she does not try to be grandiose in her independence. She turns for help when she needs it. She regards her father not as a child's oasis from reality nor as an adolescent who angrily attacks him for his weaknesses, but as an adult who can be consulted for advice in areas in which his judgment can be respected. She relates similarly to her other intimates, consulting and discussing rather than depending on or ignoring.

Women with mature self-esteem face their insecurities in order to overcome them. They realize their uncertainties are not everywhere (another way to describe low self-esteem) but only in some areas. Independent, self-confident women know there is a high price to be paid for hiding too much from insecurity. There is the danger their anxieties will spread, as the habit of automatic avoidance narrows the horizons of their lives and damages their overall self-esteem. They pay the price of discomfort as they face new situations in which they feel uncertain of successful outcome. It is only by accepting and facing challenge that it can be overcome.

Fathers can help grown-up daughters by accepting the equal status of their adult offspring and by being helpful in the right way at the right time. This may mean a little oasis solace or adolescent arguing when necessary, but always with the view toward rapid return to mature dealing. In order to participate in this adult equality daughters must accept fathers' weaknesses. The child does not see them and the adolescent totally fights and rejects them. The adult daughter may regret her father's imperfections, especially if they are numerous, but only through accepting them and putting them in perspective can she enjoy and benefit from his advice. A woman who rejects her father as stupid and his advice as totally useless may be right in some cases, but often it is the disappointed child or rebellious adolescent in her that exaggerates his imperfections. As an equal, the adult woman may be upset by childlike aspects of her father which she may choose at times to mother or even discipline, but she does not dismiss the whole man. Fathers and daughters who successfully adjust to adult equality can look forward to lifelong mutual benefit and pleasure.

The Insecurities of Adult Women

It is the rare woman (or man for that matter) in our society who is secure. The reason is the heterogeneous nature of our society and the changing roles of women. Farm families bring up women who end up as stockbrokers. Daughters schooled never to show feelings marry emotionally expressive men. Young women of formal upbringing work for informal bosses. Because of our diversity of child rearing we do not know how to read each other's nonverbal signs and signals. Because the role of the woman is rapidly changing she does not know whether to be sweet or aggressive, likable or strong, deferential or glib, reserved or seductive. Her father had no idea which role he was bringing her up to fulfill. Some roles he never imagined. It is very difficult for generations to understand, advise, and sympathize with one another when they are so different. As a result, even those women who successfully progressed through the developmental stages of self-esteem and security retain large areas in which they are uncertain and which must be overcome. Typically these uncertainties are in the areas of *overall self-esteem, changing identities, success, math,* and *lovers.*

Overall Self-esteem

It is certainly odd to think that a great number of women were properly brought up by their parents, reached adult self-sufficiency and separation, yet remain shaky overall after thirty. Seeming solid to outsiders, they are unsure within. Why? They do not know how to behave and many try to do too much.

The majority of adult women I interviewed do not want to be like their mothers or fathers. They desire to be radically different, more loving, less subservient, more capable, fulfilled, creative, successful, and happy. Many view their fathers as responsible and materially successful, but at the expense of emotional fulfillment and family closeness. Mothers they believed to be downtrodden, timid, idle, and depressed. The traditional male and female roles are seen as leading to different kinds of failure, the male in relationships and the female in career. Middle-aged men, their fathers, deny their emotions and have no real intimacy with family or friends, while their mothers idly fill the gap created by the empty nest. The adult daughter copes by delaying marriage and children in order to be successful like her father, while attempting to maintain friendships and intimacy like her mother.

It is at the point of trying to combine the male and female —success in career and in love—that strain begins and insecurity develops. Should she be nice or cutthroat, competitive or loving, mean enough to drive a hard bargain and shape up subordinates, or understanding and kind? Most women have been brought up to express the affiliative side of their natures and downplay power drives. Thus they are prepared to be nurturing mothers, not executives, to fill typically female careers, and to be insecure in jobs usually held by men.

As she progresses in her thirties her insecurity may grow and begin to threaten her overall self-esteem. The reason is a little complicated but has to be understood in order for women to realize when and why they ask too much of themselves. A simple sociological rule puts it best: *Competition breeds conformity*. To win a hundred-yard dash an athlete cannot employ a standing start but must get down in the starting blocks *just like the other contestants*. Otherwise the race will be lost. To be successful in the world of business a woman must act like the others, like men, like her father. She must deemphasize emotions and intimacy and be controlled and powerful. During the period of attempted transition to traditionally male behavior or of the decision *not* to give up the affiliative side of her nature, a woman may feel very upset and insecure. Not trained to and not willing to compete in male terms, she does not know and is not willing to do what needs to be done to succeed.

The biological clock ticks on. Serious career women want a baby in their early or mid-thirties. Some accept the male standard, take two weeks off from work to have it, get full-time help, and go back to the twelve-hour work day. Such women may end up like their own fathers but they are not insecure and their overall self-esteem is unthreatened. But many of the women I have studied are not content to turn the up-bringing of their children over to others and try to do every-thing perfectly. They attempt to combine the best attributes of their own mothers and fathers, to be loving, and to be win-ners. Those who eventually succeed pass through a stage of insecurity in their thirties as they adjust their sights. It is the compromises they must make that threaten self-esteem.

It is possible to run a respectable hundred-yard dash from a standing start, but it cannot be world class. Careers can be very satisfying combined with loving, mothering, and intimate marriage, provided a woman (or man, for that matter) accepts less than world-class status. Such resignation is painful and achieved only after much self-assessment. During the process a woman may feel very insecure and threatened in her self-esteem as she wonders whether she is a good enough worker and mother.

Yeats said a person cannot be a success at work and at life. He was correct in the unlimited sense of becoming the most prominent in one's field, while retaining loving contacts with friends and family. We like, for example, to think of presi-dents of the United States as family men, but it is largely a myth. Being out on the road alone for two years of campaign-ing hardly leaves time or energy for friends and family. If spouses are willing to follow, fine; otherwise the family never sees them. But success at work and life can be achieved if each is scaled down a bit in mind of the other. Today's women do this as pioneers attempting to successfully integrate the best attributes of traditional male and female roles. Those who try to combine the two perfectly experience insecurity and harm to their self-esteem, while those who accept less worldly success than their fathers and less availability to children than their mothers achieve a new realistically based self-esteem from the happy integration of the two roles.

CHANGING IDENTITIES

Personality is the summation of a woman's distinguishing character traits, attitudes, and habits. It is determined by conscious and unconscious factors as well as by inalterable, inherited physical and mental characteristics. There is a lot modern American women try to do with their personalities, to train, psychoanalyze, express, change, realize, and improve them. Personality traits can go out of style, leaving a fifty-year-old woman depressed and confused. No longer valued for her warm friendliness, she may be denigrated because of her vapid conversation and lack of career.

A stable society prepares a young girl for her adult role. In America a late adolescent was expected in terms of Eriksonian theory of the nineteen-fifties to choose an identity. Now women choose new identities every decade. After high school or college it is work, marriage, child rearing with career, or back to work afterward, career change, and there is the need to keep up with the rapidly evolving fads and styles broadcast by the mass media. Television and radio exert powerful influences on our personalities and behavior. Women must keep developing. All this change is exciting and interesting, and can lead to lifelong insecurity and shaky self-esteem. There is no safe and secure station for the mature older woman. She must keep dancing all her life. This is not meant to imply a stable society is better than our own. Change and evolution throughout one's life is desirable and stimulating, and keeps women intelligent and youthful. As Aristotle said, security is for the clam, for humans the exercise of the mind is the most rewarding. Insecurity may not feel good but it is desirable. Isaac Bashevis Singer speaks of the importance of suspense in a person's life. Not knowing what will happen makes for insecurity, but it also keeps up interest.

It would require a magician, not a father, to have prepared his daughter for all the unexpected adaptations she has had to make in our unpredictably changing world. The complications of modern American marriage, career, and mixing the two could not have been foreseen by any parent. If and when all this slows down, then fathers will be aware of all that will be asked of their daughters throughout their lives. They will know that women are likely to work, that they want to earn salaries comparable to men and be successful in what they do, that they may or may not want to be mothers and if so that they will have problems of mixing job and motherhood. They will prepare their daughters to thrive singly with or without children should the high rate of divorce continue.

The cultural-lag theory describes how people's attitudes and opinions follow change by fifty years. Fathers still see their little girls as pretty virgins and future mothers, not as surgeons and stockbrokers. Perhaps the curse of television will also prove a blessing, lessen the lag, and wake fathers up in less than half a century to the need for their daughters to be equipped for the modern world.

SUCCESS

While male parents do not prepare females very well to juggle motherhood and careers, they are generally less ambivalent about achievement than about sex. Starting early in school, fathers are pleased by the good grades, creativity, verbal superiority, athletic achievements, and social maturity of their daughters. Although a young girl can usually delight daddy with mental excellence, research shows him to be much less happy about her sexual progress. Few are enthusiastic about the prospect of her growing physical intimacy with boyfriends.

The majority of women I interviewed described their fathers as delighted by their success in school and in the early years of their careers. It was only when conflict arose between motherhood and further work advancement that fathers pushed for family. This caused much unhappiness in women used to having their fathers' unconditional support. They began to feel their fathers had never taken their work seriously and just wanted them to be like their mothers. Some daughters became enraged because their fathers wanted them to be nonworking housewives, thus squandering their careers and education.

The withdrawal of male parental support could be overcome, even forgiven, but the short-run effect is increased insecurity. Would she become an old maid or ruin her marriage or children if she persisted in her career? Her self-esteem is shaken if she goes against her father's will. Temporary security can be achieved by obeying him, but only at the price of development in the direction in which she herself believes. Obedient daughters in their twenties and thirties pay a price by arresting their continued growth and independence. Later they may feel resentment as their capacity to freely cope fails to develop or even atrophies.

MATHEMATICS

The fear of mathematics prevents women from successfully pursuing careers in a wide number of fields ranging from business to chemistry. To become bankers, accountants, physicists, statisticians, astronomers, stockbrokers, engineers, architects, financial consultants, and many other things, women need mathematics. Typically, females become frightened of mathematical studies somewhere in junior high school between the ages of twelve and fourteen. Although required to continue these courses in high school, the attempt is often halfhearted, the grades sometimes poor, and father allows it all to happen.

There is more and more recognition of the need for women to overcome their fear of math. Courses for women frightened by this subject are available. If women are going to work and take care of themselves they need to know mathematics. Numbers and bank accounts are not something left to husbands. Specific disability in mathematics is much more common in women than in men. This sex-related insecurity is a legacy of Victorian times. Modern adult women must no longer be either innocent child brides or only in female artistic pursuits without numbers, but must be trained to make full use of their inborn capacities rather than encouraged to fulfill a predestined role based on gender.

Fathers can help their daughters by being as interested in their mathematical success as they are in that of their sons. If they want their girls to be able to be doctors or bankers they must help them conquer the fear of math. The few natural mathematical minds of both sexes probably don't need much help from parents or teachers. But the overwhelming majority of men and women need to work at this subject in order to be able to learn and apply it. Fathers can help here more than mothers by providing encouragement and acting as an interested role model.

LOVERS

There are two types of insecurity women experience with men, the first a basic one reflecting serious deprivations throughout childhood and adolescence arising from disrupted relationships with both parents. Such severely mistreated women cannot imagine anyone of either sex loving and accepting them. Constant insecurity is their sad lot and their only hope to alleviate the pain is strong, usually pathological defenses. Most women, however, are fortunate enough to have been spared such severe lifelong trauma and suffer the second kind of insecurity, which could be called *healthy adult skepticism.*

Grown-up disbelief arises from the knowledge that a woman can be hurt very deeply if she is not careful. Fathers who have protected girls too much in the oasis have ill prepared them for adult intimacy. Expecting only the pleasures, they are not ready for the aggressions and disappointments. Those who are too naïve and childlike in their trust can be so deeply wounded they do not dare love again.

Fathers can help daughters learn to proceed slowly and carefully in their relationships with men. Healthy caution rather than paranoid mistrust must be emphasized. Rather than believing you can't trust men (except daddy, of course), women can be encouraged to proceed slowly. Instead of plunging ahead with impulsive abandon, they can size a lover up and put him to the test of time. Is he loyal? How does he treat his family and friends? Is he kind to those who are defenseless and unfortunate? Fathers teach their girls how to evaluate a man and what to look for. This instruction takes place over the years, usually indirectly and mostly by example. It is a lesson in values and in taking care of herself. A woman should neither bury her heart beneath armor so she can feel nothing, thereby denying herself the pleasure of love, nor wear it on her sleeve, leaving it open to recurrent pain and depression.

A woman must be prepared by her father for healthy insecurity, to enjoy the best while being prepared for the worst. Bringing her up to err excessively on the bright side of life leaves her childishly secure, basically trusting, but subject to the devastation of a child should her world explode. Too much emphasis on mistrust leaves her too defensive to enjoy and love, too unwilling to lose herself in the joy of intimacy with a man. Because of the present high divorce rate, romantic naïveté has been replaced for many by excessive cynicism. Such men and women are too mistrustful of one another. These young people feel that marriage cannot succeed. Fathers can help try to restore the balance, but the 40 per cent who are divorced and the many others who remain in unsatisfying marriages usually have badly shaken daughters who do not believe intimacy with a man can last. A male parent who has not gotten along well with his wife should try to help his daughter develop skills which will keep her from a similar fate. A woman is wise to be healthily skeptical rather than naïve or cynical.

OVERCOMING INSECURITY

The few completely confident people cannot face the human frailties we all possess. Most of us would find them unbearable because of their smugness. Conversely, not many individuals are completely insecure. However, almost everyone has some weaknesses. The extremes of running from their recognition or dwelling on them to the point of paralysis must be avoided in order to cope successfully. By assessing her strengths and weaknesses a woman can balance herself, using the cheer of one to offset the discomfort of the other.

There is neither time nor strength to conquer all our faults. Only the insecurities that keep us from something in our lives we desire are worth trying to overcome. The pain caused by not being able to reach realistic goals makes us try to change ourselves rather than ignore our fears. The knowledge of her own self-worth gives a woman the strength to attack her insufficiencies.

Five

RELATIONSHIPS

If you are like most women you are aware of the profound influence your father has had on your long-term relationships with lovers. The only problem is that this recognition usually is incomplete and comes too late to allow you to take effective action and avoid a lot of pain. The reason is the extreme complexity of trying to understand yourself, your male parent, your lover, and how all these interact. One obvious but often overlooked difficulty is that not all men affect you the same way. Your personality can be compared to a musical instrument in that the whole can be called a violin or clarinet but the parts can form many different notes. Although a woman can be labeled a certain type of person, various people she meets strike different tones. One man resonates her competitive note, another her dependent, a third her adult cooperative one. Her father has affected different parts of her personality in various ways. In order to understand her problems with men she must perceive the complexities of her own makeup, those of her lovers, and at what points their good and bad aspects meet. Father plays an important role in all of this because he was the first male influence on his daughter's personality, and thus has left his strong imprint on how she responds to and is affected by her lovers.

To think of a woman as a complex musical instrument sounding in different ways to different men depending upon which chords they resonate does not invalidate the dominant model used heretofore of the oasis, adolescent, and adult person, nor does it dispute the concept of transference, which focuses on how she tends to relate using her experience with previous, important, especially parental relationships, but it puts in perspective that a woman acts and feels differently with different men. Even predominantly oasis girls, for example, have adult tones which can be sounded by some men and not others.

Transference is the process by which an individual shifts feelings and attitudes derived from previous significant persons in his or her life onto new individuals. Although originally described by Freud in the context of the patient's reaction to the shadowy figure of the psychoanalyst, it is by no means solely confined to the consulting room, but is a phenomenon present in every aspect of our lives. We all transfer feelings derived from the past onto new situations. One common example of this is in the attitude between senior and junior members of a business organization. Most junior colleagues overestimate the power of their superiors while the majority of bosses underestimate the capabilities of those under them. This is similar to the child who sees the parent as all-powerful while the parent fails to respect the growing competence of his or her offspring.

Most psychoanalytic writing on transference implies that the adult personality is relatively constant and unchanging. Accordingly, if a woman was mistreated by an autocratic father she may react by hating men and seeking to discredit them. Her childhood neurotic pattern is repeated with all males no matter who the current one in her life is. In fact, according to this model, unless she changes herself through introspection or psychotherapy, she will be doomed to a repetitious pattern. A conservative theory developed in the late nineteenth and early to mid-twentieth century, one lesson it implied was, "Don't change boyfriends or especially husbands, change yourself!"

But even if the concept of transference is strictly adhered to it must not be forgotten that individual men affect the man-hating autocrat's daughter in different ways. A powerful man will resonate this particular transference note, while a weak, placid, or indecisive one will not. That is why second or third marriages do not have to echo the problems of the first even if the woman has not gained insight and changed her automatic attitudes toward and expectations of a man to whom she is intimately attached. Where lack of understanding and insight can hurt is if the woman keeps being drawn to autocratic men who affect her in the same way.

Experience in psychiatric practice and with women interviewed for this book reveals that a small percentage keep going out, living with, or marrying the same man and repeating disastrous patterns over and over but that most deliberately choose someone different. If the last lover was domineering the next is likely to be gentle and caretaking. If the previous man had a violent temper this one is liable to be patient. What is more likely to be the case is that deeper underlying, unsuspected patterns cause relationships with both aggressive and passive men to end unhappily because the woman is completely disappointed in both lovers not for the reasons she thinks, but because she cannot find her father's undying love and devotion in one man after another.

When a woman understands, for example, that she is an oasis girl used to being doted on by her father, she then has a chance to either pick her lover with this in mind or to try to change and stop requiring impossible attention from a man. The realization that she is childish is not so easy. If she always was and expects to be pampered, she may not be aware it is unreasonable. To realize she has had an infantalizing father and how it has affected her relationship to lovers, a woman must stand back and look at herself objectively. This is not easy for any of us to do.

If a woman has been divorced twice, she must be prepared to change her belief about the reasons. If she relaxes and frees herself of surface beliefs and prejudices it may become apparent that she stopped loving her husbands not because the first was bossy and the second was weak and indecisive but because of anger. Oasis girls do not experience themselves as spoiled and demanding. What they feel is the disappointments which arise from their excessive expectations. They do not believe their needs to be unjustified; instead they are outraged that he forgot their birthday, didn't listen uncritically to their tales of woe, or did not consider their slightest whim more important than his job or the family. Women who were doted on by worshiping fathers usually find their lovers to be cool and self-centered by comparison, even when they are attentive by normal standards; such women usually have no understanding that their expectations are too high.

The advantage of the oasis-to-adult model is to help a woman step back from her feelings of disappointment and outrage in order to gain perspective and begin to understand what kind of person she is, how she has been affected by the first, most important man in her life, her father, and how this is coloring her relationships with past and present lovers. With this new understanding she will be able to improve the future.

While oasis girls are the most obviously doomed to disappointment it must be remembered that there are childish aspects in all of us and that these discordant notes can be struck in our personalities most effectively by our intimates and by some of them more than others. Adolescent aspects of our personalities can lead to authority conflicts, touchiness, moodiness, idealism, and excessive romanticism which can do serious damage to long-term relationships.

Because it seems sensible to focus on problems that harm intimate involvements and because there is so much trouble in marriages and between long-term lovers, the negative aspects of childhood and adolescence tend to be overemphasized. But let us not forget about the freshness of childlike enthusiasm, the romance and excitement of adolescence, the positive remnants of our pasts that enliven our marriages and alliances. It is not automatically derisive to be thought of as childish or adolescent. Some of the most charming, creative adults are those who have preserved the positive aspects of youth.

Since even the most adult woman contains vestiges of her childhood and adolescence likely to arise during a long-term relationship and conceivably harm it, it is useful for her to understand herself and how her father has influenced her relationship to men. Her male parent may have encouraged her growth to maturity in some areas and not others. He may have made her too dependent on him and to that extent not available to her husband or lover, who may experience her as cold because of her continued attachment to her father.

Your past with your father influences your relationships all your life for both good and ill. If he strove to be your only man, effected an unrealistic standard no flesh-and-blood lover could ever duplicate, then you will have great difficulty finding someone who satisfies you. One way to estimate the degree to which your father doted on you is to think of the difference between the way he treated you and the way he behaved toward his wife, your mother. If they were not too dissimilar then perhaps you could find a man as attentive as he. If your father treated his wife and you badly then you may be unwilling to let men get very close to you. Some women do not realize how much they keep potential lovers away and experience this tendency as loneliness rather than as their own doing. Letting their guard down gradually in controlled amounts is the best way for them to overcome this problem. To the extent that your father prepared you for the adult world you will experience comfort with real men and be able to tolerate their weaknesses and enjoy their strengths. Not expecting too much you will not experience the excessive rage of disappointment, but not settling for too little you will not be taken advantage of and will be able to allow a man close enough to enjoy what you as an adult woman have a right to expect from an intimate connection.

PERSONALITY AND ITS PARTS

An angry young man exclaimed that there are two types of women: those looking for husbands and a free ride through life and those trying to compete and outstrip men. The first were overly dependent, the second stridently aggressive. His black-and-white extreme exaggeration underscores a dangerous pitfall in all thinking about the classification of personality, even psychiatric. For example, a person may be diagnosed as a passive-dependent personality. What can be overlooked is that this categorization may apply at one period in the individual's life and not at another. Proof of the difficulty in judging personality is underscored by the high rate of disagreement among psychiatrists about a given individual. If professionals have a hard time judging patients it is certainly true that we have difficulty judging each other and ourselves.

The main reason why we are hard pressed to clearly appraise ourselves is that we are so complex. The same woman can be extremely competitive, very dependent, and many other things depending on the situation. In court she may in her capacity as a lawyer aggressively cross-examine the witness, while at night she may want her husband to make the smallest decision. To the opposing lawyer she seems very hard while to her mate dependent and childish. Furthermore, different lovers can bring out these two opposing sides of her personality. One man who is cold and competitive makes her want to fight, while a second who is caretaking and kind strikes the dependent chord in her.

If outsiders experience her as totally different, how does she appear to herself? People usually judge themselves by what is uppermost in their attention during a particular time or phase of their life. A young woman may describe herself as intensely competitive when she is trying to build her career because she chooses to emphasize that aspect of her personality. After her baby is born she may become a kind, soft, caring mother and the hard-driver side of her, still there, is quiescent. A psychiatrist would diagnose her differently and she would describe herself differently in each phase.

Varying aspects of your personality engage with different lovers. While it is true you can't change yourself by changing partners it is also clear that you can emphasize different parts of yourself. It is a fact that some men bring out your best and others your worst. By understanding what parts you wish to emphasize at which times of your life, you will choose new partners wisely or negotiate delicate transitions with your present mate.

If the personality possesses extremely different and even contradictory facets, what is the thread running through that makes a person recognizable to herself and others as kind, aggressive, loyal, competitive, whatever it is we say typifies a certain woman? We can refer to a woman as an oasis girl, an adolescent, or an adult. Clearly it is the dominant theme in her life whether molded by her father, actively chosen by herself, or forced on her by society or necessity. Although many people believe and some theory stresses the notion that personality is immutable and people cannot and do not change, it would be better to say that although they remain fundamentally recognizable, they can and do change their emphasis and this can make them appear quite different.

PARTS OF THE PERSONALITY AND RELATIONSHIPS

A woman will emphasize certain parts of her personality with one lover and not another because of the way they affect each other and because of the time in her life during which they meet. She is aware that she likes and dislikes varying characteristics of her particular intimate, that she respects his intelligence but not his behavior at parties or the way he treats their son. If her values change she may no longer care so much about the very thing in him that once attracted her. If she now wants kindness and cooperation from him, rather than money and status, she may find their involvement has become very unsatisfying. Once a love relationship has existed for a reasonably long period of time it builds on the interaction and emphasis of certain facets of each partner's personality. Each considers the other a certain kind of person. There is great resistance to the idea or possibility of change.

When women say they got divorced or left a lover so they could grow it sounds on the surface like a simpleminded attempt at a solution that would require inward development not outward change. Thoughtless or impulsive people do attempt to change the inside by altering the outside. But, sometimes thoughtful and cautious women must get divorced in order to change. The reason is their roles in the marriage become fixed and they find it impossible to alter them within the context of the relationship. If the kind, motherly aspect of a woman's personality has been presented to her husband for twenty years, he may not like or tolerate the ambitious side that wants a career once the children have grown or the competitive part that does as well as he. Presented with the choice of remaining at home without a job in order to placate him, she is unable to give expression to a long suppressed important aspect of her character unless he lets her. If she does not back down, an insoluble conflict may split the marriage.

Change is difficult for all long-standing couples. It challenges their traditions and balance. Although much is made of the threat to the husband of the wife who goes back to work after many years, it is *change*, not work, that is anxiety-provoking. This can be easily understood if one imagines the opposite, the long-term career woman who decides to stop working and give full time to child rearing. Her husband might then worry about how they will get along on half the money and twice the mouths to feed and send to college. Not only men are threatened by change. Think of how a woman might react if her husband decided to give up his high-paying job as a tax lawyer in order to devote himself to writing and playing the cello. For couples to survive each must let the other try new things, even if it makes a partner nervous. It is the responsibility of the person changing the rules to reassure the one who is made upset. One cannot threaten one's intimate too much or he or she will become defensively anxious, authoritarian, or angry. The relationship becomes distant, uncomfortable, and empty if it survives at all. It takes a lot of skill, tact, and diplomacy to reassure one's partner enough so one can exercise freedom.

EIGHTY-ONE WOMEN

It is our close relationships with which we struggle most in our lives. Although our modern technical advances have been staggering, we do not seem to be doing very much better with our loved ones than the ancients did. We desperately need more knowledge of how to get along with our intimates. Disagreement, divorce, and loneliness plague our affluent lives. We are rich but we are poor in happiness.

The need for understanding is great but we cower at the task of pitting our feeble science against the complexities that influence lovers. There is no way to design a study that will satisfy the critic. Yet we must try. Our ignorance in this area is appalling and it cannot continue. Unhappiness and violence is the price we pay. It is better to suffer the scoff of cynics and to try to investigate this complicated area.

The question before us is one to which we already know the answer. Fathers affect the way daughters get along with lovers. But how much and in what manner? Do other factors override the power of his hold? As I started to spin the questions I realized the impossibility of answering them all. I would settle for the partial solution to even one of them. I decided to study eighty-one women more intensively than the hundreds of women that I talked to in an effort to learn about how their relationships with their fathers influenced those they had with their long-term lovers. These women were selected at random based on their willingness to talk to me in greater depth about how their fathers' lives affected them. I was surprised how readily women were able to talk about this subject and I appreciated their candor. The eighty-one were each extensively interviewed by me. Assessing a woman's relationship to her father and husband or male intimate requires extensive interviewing. It takes patience and tact, to help a woman relax, let down her defenses, and see her relationship with her father and husband or lover clearly.

Table I describes the habitual degree of distance between father and daughter over the years and its effect on closeness to lovers. If any of the terms in the table seem unclear I suggest you read on to where they are explained.

TABLE I

RELATIONSHIP OF FATHER TO DAUGHTER	*Number*	RELATIONSHIP OF DAUGHTER TO LOVER	*Number*
Symbiotic	18	Symbiotic	12
		Friendly	0
		Distant	0
		None	6
Friendly	15	Symbiotic	0
		Friendly	9
		Distant	6
		None	0
Distant	24	Symbiotic	0
		Friendly	3
		Distant	15
		None	6
Dead	12	Symbiotic	0
		Friendly	3
		Distant	6
		None	3
Divorced	12	Symbiotic	6
		Friendly	0
		Distant	3
		None	3

Symbiosis

In biology symbiosis refers to the permanent union between organisms each of which depends on the other for its existence. Psychologically it describes two people involved with one another in such a way that they cannot get along separately. Fathers and daughters who hold on to each other tightly are usually not conscious of it. Aware only of the anger, fighting, and disappointments, they do not recognize their intense dependence on one another. None of the women interviewed said straight out that she could not survive without her father. Instead everyone complained of his interference, his uninvited advice, and his resentment if she failed to call or visit.

None of the eighteen women who had excessively close ties to their fathers were able to achieve normal intimacy with husbands or lovers. They either entered into another symbiotic association or were so upset by closeness to a man that they remained alone and lonely. All eighteen had had involvements with their lovers or husbands in which they re-created the *intensity* experienced with their fathers. These relationships were characterized by much fighting and disappointment, and the women suffered as much with their husbands and lovers as they had with their male parents. The six whose relationships had come to an end missed being close to a man. Their loneliness was extremely painful and they were barely able to tolerate it. Without father or lover these victims of too-intense intimacy could not get along.

Why didn't all just continue in happy symbiosis? The reason is the happy oasis of pretty three-year-old and proud father cannot continue into adulthood. Angry fights, bickering, power struggles, and demands become the norm. Infuriated daughters of symbiosis move miles away but those who are fixated at this level find it extremely difficult to truly break away and feel free and happy far from home. They try to re-create the same intensity with a lover or husband, only to end in the same rancor. They cannot live with or without a man unless they change.

To change, a woman must first recognize her trouble and its source. It is not so easy when furious with her annoying father to realize how much she needs him. It took Carol Stern several years in therapy to stop complaining about him and to recognize how lonely and anxious she became if she did not see him for a few days.

Carol Stern is twenty-seven years old, married, and the mother of two tiny boys. Her academic record had been outstanding, a source of pride to her and her father. He is very successful in real estate and calls her up all the time or flies in for frequent visits. Carol's parents' marriage is on the verge of divorce and her mother telephones in tears and talks for more than an hour.

Because of her father's wealth and knowledge of real estate, Carol has consulted him on the purchase of her home, has used his money for the down payment and his connections for discounts on a furnace, washer, dryer, and other necessary items to furnish it. She makes no major decisions without talking to him first.

His help is not what bothers her and she is unaware of the depth of her need for it. What she complains of is his interference. He has opinions on everything in her life and voices them freely and often. What she wants is his aid when she wants it and on her terms. What she gets is a man who feels he has a right to her time and attention because she is his child and because she owes it to him, especially after all he has done for her.

Carol slowly began to understand she might have to make a choice either to accept the bad with the good in her intense tie to her father or to back off from both. She decided to do the latter but found it very difficult. Her father did not like it and she herself missed his financial and emotional support.

The effect on her marriage was interesting. Her symbiotic attachment to her husband had been so complete she scarcely noticed him. This allowed him to work almost constantly to build up his own business. They had an unstated agreement that Carol would attend to the domestic side of their lives in partnership with her father, while Jim, her husband, worked all the time. But as Carol backed off from her paternal tie she sought Jim's advice more. As she seemed more interested in him he began to work less and their marriage became more emotionally fulfilling.

Once having recognized her need a woman like Carol must then grow up. It means learning to do for herself much of what her father did for her. Not transferring her whole bag of dependencies to her husband or lover, she must handle them herself. Only then will the rage she feels that her infantile wishes are not being cared for by her male intimate subside. Her severe childlike resentments will continue to poison her relationships to men until she becomes self-sufficient and self-assured.

Distant

When fathers are distant from daughters it is difficult for women to form a symbiotic relationship with their husbands or lovers. Only three women were able to improve on their distant relationships with their fathers and create closer emotional bonds to their husbands. Typically, warmth and intimacy were so important to them and they felt so starved for it by their fathers that they deliberately picked husbands who were more emotionally available.

The other twenty-one daughters of remote fathers were not able to overcome the pattern of distance. Most had distant relationships with their husbands or lovers and some had no men at all. The fathers of the six without men were not only distant and absent, they were extremely autocratic and cruel when present. These women stayed far away from men, even though one of them thought at times she was looking for a partner. She recounted much effort in singles bars shyly and painfully talking to men. What she did not realize is that the time she enjoyed most was spent with her mother. When she felt lonely and in need of a boost at the age of thirty-five she went to have a cup of tea with her mother.

Daughters of distant fathers learn not to expect much from men. They stand on their own two feet, convinced that depending on a man is useless and inevitably leads to disappointment. Many of these women are independent, self-sufficient, and capable. They trust in their own work and efforts. This kind of woman was the most common in my sample. Not having a close relationship with her male parent led her to expect her husband or lover to be similarly distant and not to look for much pleasure or fulfillment from males. She learned to rely on herself and to look for rewards coming from her own work efforts. In fact, many of these women were successful in their chosen careers.

But most of their relationships with husbands and lovers were unhappy because they felt lonely and unable to share intimacy. Never having had the experience of comfortable closeness and warmth with their fathers, they could not achieve it with their own men. A growing girl cannot practice being a woman with a father who is not there physically and emotionally. She has no experience winning his smile, suffering his discipline, or being guided by his teaching. Men are strangers and she finds it hard to change the pattern.

The daughter of a distant father can learn to be close to men once she conquers her psychological scars. One of these is anger. Furious with father for his indifference, she sees all men as prepared to use her, but unwilling to meet her needs. Another is having grown up in a world of women close to her mother, unfamiliar and unprepared for male aggression, competition, and demand, she has no childhood or adolescent experience in winning over, arguing against, or trying to manipulate her father. Because of this she cannot negotiate well with her husband or lover and when things go wrong between them she has no facility in compromise and conflict resolution. Her only recourse is to withdraw. The result is feeling lonely and unhappy just as she did when a child.

To overcome the three scars of anger, withdrawal, or hiding in a career a woman must decide that intimacy with a man is worth having and that she wants to overcome her loneliness. Those who truly want to be close to a man must learn and practice the skills never developed with their fathers. They must accept the status of beginners and recognize their difficulty in relating to men. Those who are prepared to learn will find the pleasure of intimacy is worth the pain of achieving it. You must expose yourself gradually as you stop hiding by withdrawal or work, become close, and risk the dangers of vulnerability. Anger will be dissipated as you find your lover is not withdrawn, distant, and uninvolved as was your father, but desires to be warm and close to you.

The Right Distance

One of the hardest things in intimate human relationships is maintaining the correct interpersonal distance, not so far as to be lonely and uninvolved, not so close as to be intrusive and symbiotic. Once achieved the involvement is never fixed but fluctuates, sometimes too near, other times too far. The tie between father and daughter is always changing in the best of circumstances—close when a little girl, distant at times in adolescence, strained when she breaks away to lead her own life. Her needs, his attentions, their interactions, fluctuate as their two life cycles touch, clash, fulfill, and disappoint.

The varying degrees of intimacy between father and daughter at different points in the life cycle serve as a model for women in their long-term connections with husbands and lovers. Many marriages, for example, go through a stage of near-symbiosis in the beginning when young couples are practically inseparable, become strained and distant during early child rearing and career building, and then function at a more comfortable level of intimacy when the children are older. Women who have successfully negotiated the varying degrees of connection to their fathers are better prepared for the difficult adjustments required in long-term attachments to their lovers and husbands.

Only fifteen of the eighty-one fathers and daughters seemed to strike the right interpersonal distance, at least most of the time, and these were the women most likely to achieve comfortable intimacy with a man in their adult lives. Although fewer than 20 per cent were lucky enough to have an ideal paternal upbringing, it does not mean the remaining 80-plus per cent are doomed to miserable love lives. For one thing there are many other male influences shaping a woman such as her brothers, relatives, teachers, classmates, coworkers, friends, and lovers. There is the extraordinary capacity of humans to learn, adjust, and overcome childhood deprivations. Secondly, although the overwhelming majority of father-daughter relationships could be classified as problematic, they are not nor do they necessarily produce pathological attachments to lovers and husbands. Because a woman tries to be too close or is too far from her lover is not a sickness. But it is something she needs to understand before she can adjust it, and awareness of the paternal antecedent helps. A woman who was distant from her father and automatically so from her lover or spouse can recognize the symptoms of loneliness and isolation by herself and make the effort to become closer and more emotionally involved or to find someone else with whom she can be warmer. She must be able to recognize the symptoms of too much or too little intimacy in her adult relationships. Once she understands that her fighting and anger toward her husband or lover comes from symbiosis, from too much dependency and expectation or that her loneliness and depression comes from lack of emotional sustenance in her adult attachment, she is in a position to adjust the degree of intimacy rather than blindly repeat or react against a parental pattern.

This reading of herself is very complicated. For example, a woman may feel lonely, realize she was brought up by a cool and distant father, and decide she wants more intimate involvement with her husband only to discover as she gets closer to him that she feels too intruded upon and her privacy invaded. The prototype of her lack of emotional intensity learned with father and continued in her marriage is a style with which she feels most comfortable and her loneliness would be best relieved by taking a job and working with others or by seeing her friends. Or conversely, a woman whose attachment to her male parent was symbiotic and who decides she is tired of possessive, jealous, and demanding men and that she wants a cooler one may discover she feels isolated and lonely in an affair or marriage in which there is greater distance. We all at times long for a different interpersonal intensity—more warmth, more independence—only to find we do not really want it.

Not every woman wants the same intensity of involvement in her intimate relationship with a man. It is important to remember that the appetite for closeness is as variable as the one for food or sex. The widely believed notion that there is a correct amount of intimacy one should have is as silly as the belief that there is a right number of times a week to have sexual intercourse. Each woman must decide what degree of closeness to a man is right for her. One good way to make this decision is to decide what feels right for you. If you are neither angry nor lonely chances are you are at the right interpersonal distance *for you*. But remember, your needs change. You may want more involvement with your lover at one stage of your life than at another. Couples that do best can adjust to the varying needs of each partner and adapt the degree of caring and intimacy to fit the situation. They are not tyrannized by rigid expectations about distance or intimacy but move together and apart as needed, making their needs known and meeting those of the other person. For women intimate relationships change over time with their lovers as they did with their fathers. The sensitive monitoring of and adjustment of interpersonal distance is a major ingredient in achieving a satisfying and long-lasting loving connection.

Dead or Divorced Fathers

There are twenty-four women whose fathers were either dead or divorced, twelve in each group. A look at Table I shows the effect on their adult relationships to be quite varied. Obviously the age at which the loss occurs, the quality of the relationship beforehand, and the effect on the mother (e.g., severe depression, solid remarriage) are powerful fac-

tors. It is of interest that the six women who had no relationship with a man at all were younger as a group when
their fathers disappeared by death or divorce. In the divorced
group six women formed symbiotic relationships with their
lovers and none could achieve the Right Distance, while no
woman whose father died formed a symbiotic relationship.
These suggest that the daughters of the divorced tend to hold
too tightly to their men or remain safely distant, but are unable to achieve comfortable closeness. The daughters of the de-
ceased, on the other hand, seem to shun symbiosis for fear of
losing their mate as they did their father. Only three of the
twenty-four in this group were able to form comfortably intimate relationships, which illustrates the powerful effect of
these traumas on a woman's ability to relate to men.

Five patterns with lovers emerged as a result of absent fathers: the Frenetic Searchers, the Hopeless, the Clingy, the
Awkward, and the Distrustful. The *Frenetic Searchers* were
unable to get over the loss of their fathers and seemed to find
and lose him over and over again. They would make an intense relationship with a new lover in which each was totally
preoccupied with the other only to break up after a short
time. The loss threw them into the depths of despair from
which they rapidly recovered when infatuated with a new
man. By going from one lover to the next they repeated the
trauma of losing the first man—their father—and by finding a
new attachment they undid the loss by replacing him with
someone else. Such women are on a romantic rollercoaster
from despair to elation. One woman tried to emphasize the
pleasure of the search while limiting the pain of the loss by
rarely making dates by phone, although she was very attractive and had many calls. Instead she would go to places
where she knew attractive men might be—dances, parties,
private clubs, and even singles bars. She became excited as

she searched for a new man and when she found him she would have a brief affair often only one night in duration. In this way she emphasized the pleasure of restoration and minimized the pain of loss.

The *Hopeless* usually lost their fathers earlier or even more traumatically, for they have no hope at all as do the Searchers. Expecting to find nothing they are paralyzed by despair. They dare not hope because they either know they will be disappointed or cannot risk the emotional pain should they be left again. These women are distrustful of relying at all on a man and feel sure he will treat them badly. If they are well adjusted they fill their lives with careers, friends, and other interests and experience little distress from not having a man of their own, but if they are less defended they can feel isolated and very alone. These unhappy women need to build a life in which they find solace in other pursuits or to learn to trust a man slowly and by degrees. Many are able to overcome their hopelessness, but not without a lot of effort.

The *Clingy* try to make up for the past. One attractive twenty-two-year-old woman whose father deserted her when she was eighteen months old boasted of not having been out of her boyfriend's sight for two years. They lived and worked together. Fortunately this meshed with his needs and the relationship continued to fulfill them both. But when clinging dependence is not gratified as it cannot be in most instances women can suffer a lot. They feel angry, fearful, depressed, and disappointed because their needs are considered excessive by their partners and not met. They may drift from one affair to another enjoying the beginning time of infatuation as an opportunity to cling more. The ones who do not get over this need become bitter as one man after another disappoints them. They may give up on sexual relationships and either tightly hold their children or turn to a career for satisfaction.

Some need psychiatric help while others are able to mature as a result of repeated experience to the point where they can enjoy realistic ties to a man and take what pleasure is maturely available.

The *Awkward* have been deprived of a model in their male parent and do not know how to behave in an intimate relationship with a man. These women are not as emotionally damaged as the previous types and their naïveté tends to diminish as they grow older. Having been deprived through the death or divorce of their father they have difficulty with men early on. Some are taken advantage of because of their lack of experience, while others fail to sustain what started out a good intimate involvement because of their lack of skill. But these women have the least trouble overcoming their difficulty; it is often simply a matter of time.

The *Distrustful* are cynical and expect all men to desert them after the honeymoon. They are unimpressed by flowers, attention, and courtship and wonder what will happen when infatuation wanes. Women whose fathers divorced their mothers feel this way. In fact no woman of the twelve divorced fathers was able to establish comfortable distance from her man. She either clung in symbiosis, was distant, or avoided men altogether. This is a small group and I hesitate to say that no woman whose parents are divorced will be able to establish the kind of long-term attachment to a man which will satisfy her needs. I suspect many eventually will. But in this time of an escalating high divorce rate women realistically worry about the permanence of their marriages and love affairs.

The effect on a woman of the death of her male parent is more difficult to generalize about. In the group I studied it varied with the kind of relationship that existed beforehand and her age at the time of his death. Those who had success-

fully progressed through the stages of development with their
fathers only to have them die when they were in their late
teens or early twenties seemed not to suffer ill effects excessively. If the daughter was very young or the relationship
with him was disturbed, the scar can be serious. But such a
woman can help herself by looking at her attachment to her
father systematically as I have suggested. Through understanding her emotional involvement with him before his
death she can begin to counteract its effect.

THE EFFECT OF STERN AND GENTLE FATHERS

The fifty-seven women (excluding twenty-four whose fathers
were dead or divorced) rated their fathers as to whether they
were stern or gentle. It should be remembered that a father
who appears mild around his wife may be very commanding
outside the home. Table II lists fathers as strong or weak and
rates the effect on their daughters' long-term involvements
with men.

TABLE II

| | Relationships with Men | |
	Happy	Unhappy
Stern Father	10	16
Gentle Father	23	8

Stern fathers had a negative effect on their daughters' relationships with men. Only ten of the twenty-six women enjoyed
fathers were described as weaker than their wives, and twenty-
comfortable intimacy with their lovers or husbands. Thirty-one

three of these women were currently in happy relationships. Perceiving her father as kind and gentle in the home has a more positive effect on the way a woman relates to men in her adult life. It must be remembered that perception is the key word here, since there is no objective evidence that these fathers were in fact strong, weak, kind, or cruel. It would be extremely difficult to get at the truth since one child may view a father as strong or cruel, while a brother or sister experiences him in a different way.

If you have a harsh father at home, you might be either afraid of men or spend your life trying to please them. The daughters of severe fathers in the home sometimes have poor relationships with lovers because they try to please men while building up suppressed anger. Women should try to reach a kindly feeling toward their fathers if they do not already have one. It will help them relate to men. By not perceiving your father as austere and frightening but as approachable and loving, you will relate better to men.

The gentle father provided a warm oasis, and the woman who experienced this comfortable love will have the best long-term relationship with a man. All of these women were also successful in their careers. The fathers, then, did not allow their daughters to become arrested in the oasis but encouraged them to be independent and successful. Because their gentle, loving fathers had encouraged them to develop their own strengths, every one of them was powerful in the world, but kept herself sufficiently reined in at home to maintain a good marriage. The eight daughters whose relationships to men were unsatisfactory had a spouse who was inferior to her and jealously tried to control and police her social behavior. The others were married to strong equals, but treated the home as an oasis rather than a competitive arena.

If you saw your father as gentle at home with your mother, you will consider men safe. Just the reverse is true in your career in that it is the daughters of men who are strong themselves, in their own careers, who tend to be successful. A man who is not harsh with his wife will not be so with his daughter either. Such women find men unthreatening supports at home and are able to lead in their careers. The typical American male is powerful in his career and comes home and relaxes. He brings up a daughter who is not frightened of him and knows how to lead, a talent that serves in her career and in her intimate home life.

RELATIONSHIP TYPES

Since women's personalities are complex and affected by different men in various ways, the type of relationship a woman develops with a particular man is influenced by who he is and at what point in their lives they meet. A woman may lean on a warm, caretaking man and be competitive with one who strives for power. She may be dependent in her childbearing years and distant when trying to succeed in her career. In spite of this variation with different men and at various phases of her life, an attachment can be looked at at a given moment and described as primarily of a certain type.

One of the great stresses in relationships is when one or both partners wish to change emphasis from one mode of interaction to another. Tired of dependence, they might seek distance and freedom. Lonely and separate, they might desire warmth and intimacy. Any change between partners can cause anxiety. What will it mean if they do not relate in the same old distant way? Will increased intimacy mean loss of

freedom, interference, being swallowed up? Or will less closeness and dependency lead to complete abandonment? If
fear of change hinders the necessary adjustments needed for
the alliance to survive, then so does resentment. "After all I've
done for you, how dare you withdraw from me?" Anger prevents cooperation if both people feel shortchanged. The hostility polarizes the role of each mate and makes each unwilling to adapt for the survival of the relationship.

Most women are capable of all the relationship styles which
will be described. Some are acutely aware of how they interact while others are completely unconscious. It is possible for
a woman to fill her life with diversion and pay little attention
to how she relates to her lover. Recognition of which is your
dominant style is necessary in order for you to change it
should you so desire.

Dependent

Modern women do not like this kind of relationship any-
more. They want to use their education, realize their potential, and have their own money. The old-fashioned wife who
asked her husband for a new dress is not for them. Those who
are unable to care for themselves can be left poor and helpless or must cling no matter how they are treated by their
mate. Dependency is not a good idea for women. It is much
better to be strong and self-sufficient. Equal relationships between men and women have become the rule.

But what about the dependent wishes and needs in all of
us? What about the desire to be cared for, to be protected, to
be relieved of the unpleasant aspects of hard decision making
and recognition of the sad aspects of life? These dependent
wishes are in all people—men and women—and they cause a

good deal of trouble in long-term relationships. The awareness, for example, that she has worked hard all day or had a difficult time with the children and therefore *deserves* to have her wishes gratified gives a person a feeling of righteous claim on her mate's services. The belief that one's partner owes her something gives angry force to her expectations and demands.

Men, of course, are dependent just as often as women, perhaps more so. Having been cared for by their mothers, they expect their wives and girlfriends to do the same. Some can barely do anything for themselves except earn a living. But they feel money gives them the right to be waited on.

Fear of dependency is almost as big a problem as dependency itself—perhaps even bigger. It prevents partners from allowing themselves to get close so as to enjoy the other person. For some it means never being really married, except in name. People who are not sure of their own maturity often confuse adult dependence with the childlike variety. Usually they do so because their development has been arrested by overly indulgent parents or because they were deprived by neglectful ones and thus retain strong infantile needs as grown-ups. For them leaning on a loved one activates deep infantile longings, which are doomed to disappointment in adulthood. Letting themselves become aware of and indulge wishes to be cared for exposes them to a sense of helplessness and/or the danger of abandonment. It also opens them to rages of disappointment, which might possibly drive the needed person away. Paradoxically, extremely dependent women can act as though completely self-sufficient out of fear. Superficially they appear so strong that they seem admirable. But a closer look reveals how needful they are.

A thirty-year-old woman who lived alone and worked a

marathon week had been so dependent on the only two men she allowed herself to be close to in the past that when the first left she became totally unable to function for over a year, and by the time the second had deserted she had allowed him to abuse her for much of the two years they had been together in an effort to keep him. As a result of these experiences she gave men up and turned to her career until one winter when she went skiing. While sharing a ski house with a large group of men and women, she became aware one night of how much she wanted one of the men to hold her and when he made no attempt to do so she became extremely depressed and remained so for many months.

The fear of dependency or of acknowledging the wish is a problem for all men and women. The cynical expect nothing and the naïve want too much care. Early-childhood and adolescent experiences strongly influence the amount a woman requires from her mate and how much she trusts she will receive. Whenever adjustments occur and one partner wishes to become less dependent, the other one feels threatened, abandoned, and angered and tries to resist. Dependent couples can hold each other in a vise from which there is no escape except by splitting up. The reproach of the one upsets the other too much. Neither is willing to let the other grow.

Overcoming excessive dependency in a relationship is a slow and difficult process. The woman has both herself to deal with and her partner's need to keep her the same. It is hard enough to get the courage to go out and seek a job, a promotion, new friends, to try new sports or community activities without a vote of confidence from her mate. If he insists she be dependent and not work, if he becomes upset when she is not at home during the day for him to call, then her efforts to be self-sufficient and seek new interests lead to conflict.

The woman stuck in dependency and trying to grow out of it needs help from friends and relatives. Realizing her husband is threatened may make her angry at him but if she values the marriage she should try to reassure him and be as sympathetic as possible. The difficulty is she is not very sure of herself at a time when she is gathering her courage to try new things and finds it hard to feel sorry for the man who is trying to stop her efforts. But if the couple realizes it is best that they let each other go a little, then they will give and receive the freedom they would otherwise have to split to gain.

A woman's problems with dependency are strongly influenced by her relationship to her father. Those who had everything done for them find it hard to forgive their lover's failure to do the same. Women who have been spoiled by their male parents have a hard time in equal relationships. Naturally they do better when their husbands or lovers are older and take care of them. Adolescent-like females are caught in their conflict between being dependent and breaking away and are likely to fight in order to achieve self-sufficiency. Their relationships can be stormy, especially at a time when they feel restrained. Women whose fathers have helped them become fully mature are less likely to get into dependent relationships, although they sometimes do. This is most likely in those whose fathers have rushed them into adulthood, shortchanging them on the oasis and adolescence years. Such women have deep deprivations which can catch them unawares.

Since adults need people to satisfy their adult needs, they are in fact dependent on them. This is especially true of the person with whom they are most intimate. The psychoanalyst Fairbairn wisely defined maturation as a progression from infantile dependence to mature dependence. In this respect dependence is the opposite of narcissism, not of self-reliance. Relying on an intimate is not the same as infantile or neurotic helplessness. The woman who can make this distinction will be able to enjoy her lover free of the extremes of childhood rage should she expect too much, or of lonely isolation should she expect nothing. The helplessness of infantile dependence harms intimacy, while the nurturing of mature dependence promotes it. Such couples are not afraid of becoming childlike if they are close, nor do they become constantly angry because of unmet excessive demands, but are able to enjoy the pleasure to be had in a grown-up, successful relationship.

INTIMACY IN THE NINETEEN-EIGHTIES

It is my impression from clinical experience and from the eighty-one women I have carefully studied that the predominant relationship style of the nineteen-eighties is one that would in the past have been called distant. Distance is defined not so much by how much time is spent together as it is by what a woman expects from the man to whom she is closest. If her only wish is for a companion on formal occasions and not for a confidant with whom to share her most intimate secrets, then the relationship is cold and separate. Those in distant relationships do not expect much in the way of sharing or emotional contact. They are in the business of marriage or of living together, but they are not close. To them marriage is corporate, not warm and involving. The main reason why the predominant relationship style of the nineteen-eighties has become distant is the high divorce rate. Women rely less on their husbands and more on developing their own careers and potential. They do so not out of narcissism but from a protective, healthy retreat from depending on others. If distant relationships remain the norm then perhaps it is old-fashioned to call warm, friendly, or even competitive intimacy the right distance. Table III shows how the eighty-one I studied fall in terms of how they relate to their husbands or lovers:

TABLE III

RELATIONSHIP TO HUSBAND OR LOVER

Symbiotic	18
The right distance	15
Distant	30
None	18

Just because distance is the norm and in that sense normal does not make it desirable emotionally. That well over half (59 per cent) of those interviewed had either a distant or no relationship at all to a man left many of the women lonely or searching elsewhere to fulfill their needs. They buried themselves in their careers, turned to friends and relatives for support, or became involved in adulterous liaisons. Those who worked all the time did not always do so as a reaction to neglect by their husbands or lovers. Many shared what was heretofore primarily the man's pattern, the sincere enjoyment of a challenging career, and limited their emotional involvement at home by choice.

Their relationships to their fathers strongly influenced the distant ones they had with their lovers. Of the thirty distant women only six were close to their fathers. Table IV shows this:

TABLE IV

*Relationship to Fathers of Thirty Women Who Were Distant
from Their Lovers*

RELATIONSHIP TO FATHERS

Right distance	6
Distant	15
Dead or divorced	9

This table emphasizes the powerful effect her experience
with father has on a woman's involvement with her lovers.

One implication of these findings is the decline in family
closeness described in the Carnegie Report on child rearing.*
Fathers are not close to daughters and daughters are not
warmly intimate with lovers. There is an increased tendency
to rely on oneself and look less to a relationship for comfort
and solace. There is nothing intrinsically good or bad about
how involved one is with people, provided one is not left
lonely and empty.

An attempt was made to rate the eighty-one women carefully as happy or unhappy. Admittedly this is an inexact
measure and the decision was made on the basis of their predominant mood over many days and weeks rather than that
of a single day. Of the group thirty-three were unhappy, dissatisfied with their lives and relationships, and forty-eight
were more or less productive and content. Table V shows the
degree of closeness to their lovers and husbands of the two
groups.

* *All Our Children: The American Family under Pressure,* by Kenneth
Keniston and the Carnegie Council on Children (New York: Harcourt
Brace Jovanovich, 1977).

TABLE V

Happiness as a Function of Distance from Lover

DISTANCE FROM LOVER		PER CENT
Unhappy 33		
Symbiotic	6	33%
Right distance	3	20%
Distant	6	20%
None	18	100%
Happy 48		
Symbiotic	12	66%
Right distance	12	80%
Distant	24	80%

A most striking finding is that being distant from her man did not make a woman unhappy. In fact, 80 per cent of the women who were not close to their husbands and lovers were content. This finding seems to contradict psychoanalytic theory and other psychological schemes that connect satisfaction with closeness and intimacy and distance with unhappiness. However, since—as will be seen in the next section—80 per cent of the women in distant relationships committed adultery, they were fulfilling their needs elsewhere.

What is also striking is that all eighteen women with no intimate relationship were unhappy. It seems that it is not how close or far but that the partner exists that is important to a woman's well-being. On the other hand, 80 per cent of the group who enjoyed intimacy at the "right distance" were happy as they were supposed to be theoretically, as were two thirds of those in symbiotic relationships.

In conclusion, women can be happy with any degree of closeness to or distance from their lovers just so long as they have one. There is no proper interpersonal distance from a man that ensures contentedness, although those in distant relationships turn to other people or activities for emotional sustenance. Each woman must find the degree of intimacy or its lack with which she is comfortable. Encouraging couples to do more things together to increase their closeness is unwise, unless they do not agree and one wants symbiosis while the other wants distance. Distant relationships can give the freedom to pursue career, family, or leisure time interests. It all depends on whether partners agree on how much involvement they want whether they are content with their lives.

ADULTERY (THE ADJUSTOR OF INTERPERSONAL DISTANCE)

Whether or not a married woman commits adultery does not only reflect on her own psychology; it is a sign of how she is getting along with her husband. Twenty-four out of thirty married women (80 per cent) whose relationships were distant had sexual affairs. They were asked why and gave two reasons: the need for closeness, more attention, intensity, and caring, and the search for excitement and relief from marital boredom. Since women whose marriages sustain them emotionally are usually not bored, the second reason probably is a byproduct of the first. Boredom can be a symptom of depression and women whose marriages do not provide emotional warmth turn to love affairs to supplement what they are not getting at home.

Half of the women in symbiotic relationships (nine of eighteen) also committed adultery. Why? To get away from the stifling possessiveness of their partners and get some distance. Only 20 per cent (three of fifteen) of those in correct-distance relationships took a lover.

TABLE VI

Adultery and Type of Relationship to Husband

ADULTERY	TYPE OF RELATIONSHIP TO HUSBAND	
	Distant	80%
36	Symbiotic	50%
	Right distance	20%

Adulterous relationships, although motivated by many complicated factors, adjust intimacy. When not emotionally sustained by her husband a woman seeks caring elsewhere and when too involved she finds another man to help her move away. Correct-distance marriages, however, are rarely complicated by infidelity. A woman feels loved and supported without being smothered. This suggests that a wife who takes a lover should pay attention to her marriage. She is probably not satisfied with the way she relates to her husband. The most likely cause is emotional neglect and the second most likely is excessive demand.

Barbara Pleasants is thirty-two years old and has been married to John for eight years. They have two children. Recently she began working toward her master's degree in fine arts and started an affair with her professor of Italian Renaissance painting. John and Barbara had drifted far apart. An ambitious middle manager hoping to make it to the top of a large corporation, he worked long hours. What little free time he had he spent racing sailboats with his friends. His wife rarely saw him and when she did the conversation was forced. Their sex life was infrequent and not much fun. The professor was vastly different. They talked for hours, sharing interests and ideas. Their lovemaking was an exciting outgrowth of their closeness. Barbara had found an answer to what she was not getting from her marriage.

There was a strange echo in her behavior. Her father had always been around. They did many things together. Her husband was clearly her father's inferior, less successful both in the business world and with her. She adored her father as she did her professor. She began to realize that marrying her husband kept father number one with her. Her affair meant she was finally ready to supplant father.

Helen Morris, on the other hand, could not get space to breathe. Her husband worked many of his office hours at home and was always around. He loved to lecture her about his ideas on how to bring up the children and on what she should do to handle the office politics and problems she encountered in her job in a small accounting firm. No subject was too petty for his attention. He advised her and he tried to think for her. His efforts made her feel like a child. They infringed on her freedom and made her believe he regarded her as unable to think for herself. Her lack of gratitude for his help made her feel guilty. Beginning her affair with a manager at the office made her even more so.

When she was seven years old Helen's mother divorced her father. She saw little of him afterward. Her husband's excessive attentions had been very welcome at first. Helen believed she did not know what to do or how to behave and Tom's advice seemed necessary. Having grown up without a father she felt the need for a man's care. But after six years of Tom's suggestions she had had enough. The man in the office who thought Helen extremely intelligent seemed very attractive. To be admired rather than treated like a child was uplifting. Helen felt much better. She decided to separate from Tom.

Women do not want too little or too much attention. While people naturally differ in the amount of involvement they wish with their spouse or lover, most require a reasonable degree of sustenance in their marriages. When they do not get it they are likely to turn to affairs.

COMPETITION

Couples usually compete on some level, in their careers, in sports, for dominance, to avoid unpleasant tasks, intellectually, sexually, socially, over the children, for attention, for love. In fact, some experts believe that one main cause of marital difficulties is that Americans grow up in a competitive environment for grades, in sports, in business, and are unprepared for the cooperative equality required to make long-term intimate relationships work. Competition is a large source of disappointment and disturbance to men and women who had hoped their homes would provide a rest from the realities and rivalries of the workaday world.

The degree to which competition dominates a woman's intimate love life is largely determined by the relationship she had with her father. Daughters of autocratic men have a lot of fight in them. Having been ordered about they struggle for dominance in their marriages and love affairs. So too are women who are used to having their own way with their fathers. They expect their husbands to cater to them and struggle with them if they do not. The level of maturity a woman has reached with respect to her father is very important. Oasis girls do not compete when pampered but do so in rela-

tionships with immature boys. Adolescent women struggle
with authority and with their lovers and husbands. Needing
to assert themselves against the perceived authority of the
man with whom they live, they are neither independent nor
able to stand fully on their own.

Sometimes the most competitive women marry or choose
lovers who are so far away from sources of possible strife that
peace prevails. A young, extremely competitive woman might
choose an old, kind, soft man, for example. Where she would
fight with someone her own age she gets along with him.
Relationships in which oasis girls are dependent on caretaking, fatherlike (not necessarily older) husbands and lovers
usually do not result in too much competition.

Adult women can be competitive or not, depending on the
degree of maturity they have reached. Those who are not so
sure of their powers may struggle, while those who are
confident delight in the lovers' achievements. It must be
remembered that adult level is not achieved at age thirty fully
and forever, but that the maturation process continues
throughout the thirties, forties, and fifties. The unsure adult
who fearfully conforms to that which her father once ordered
her to do is much more ready to fight when her nervous order
is threatened, while the creatively independent woman certain of her own standards need not struggle so readily with
her man. She is much more likely to pick one who fits well
with her standards and to respect his individuality as she expects him to respect hers.

THE CORRECT DISTANCE

The correct distance can be defined as one which provides
enough emotional contact and warmth to be fulfilling and not

so much as to stifle and destroy freedom and privacy. Human beings have two simultaneous needs which are in opposition to one another: the need for being with people and the need for being alone. As one of these is being satisfied the desire for the other grows. Thus, the longer one is alone, the more the need to be in someone's company is felt and the longer one is with people, the greater the desire for solitude becomes. The correct distance between lovers is always changing. Furthermore, it is very hard to measure. It is best achieved when both partners agree on what it should be. A man desiring symbiosis does not do well with a woman wanting distance.

People in long-term relationships frequently readjust the distance between them. For a woman to be happy at the correct distance from her husband or lover she must be prepared for fluctuations in their involvement and not get too upset when things cool down. The often reported sexless periods in twenty- to thirty-year marriages are an extreme example of this. Sometimes representing anger and at others preoccupations with personal problems or strivings, these chaste times are an effort to achieve distance. Yet these couples do not necessarily have remote marriages overall. It is merely a phase.

Ideally the correct distance works best for mature couples since it gives them the warmth they need, while allowing the freedom of an independent existence. Twelve of the fifteen women who believed their relationships possessed this comfortable degree of intimacy described themselves as happy about their attachment. They were involved enough to draw sustenance from the relationship while still free to work and achieve in the outside world. Unfortunately, only fifteen of the eighty-one women interviewed felt their relationships provided the kind of intimacy they wanted.

Since 80 per cent (twenty-four of thirty) of the distant and 66 per cent (twelve of eighteen) of the symbiotic also believed themselves happy, it may be that the *true* correct distance is what people want in their lives, not what a theoretical discussion indicates they should desire. The only argument against this is the frequency of adultery in these two groups. Our relationships seem to be moving in the direction of less intimacy. Perhaps we are moving *out* of a romantic age and into a classic one. In a nineteenth-century romantic opera when the hero left the heroine she jumped from the castle parapet to her death, whereas in an eighteenth-century classic opera she found another lover. Less emotional intensity may not be a sign of declining civilization and narcissism, but simply a calmer, more practical way to live.

FEAR OF FAMILY REPETITION

While interviewing women regarding the effect their fathers had on their long-term intimate relationships with lovers I made a surprising discovery. Time and time again their choice of men was motivated by the fear of repeating family patterns. Behind some of these fears, Freud's dictum asserts, a wish can be discerned. Thus the woman who vows never to marry a materialistic man like her father and live in a similar suburb may end up with a carbon copy. What is common to both the fear and the wish is the strong hold father has on you which makes you either fear being like him or its opposite—desire to emulate his life. "I want a man just like dad" is very close psychologically to "I do not want a man anything like him."

More women are aware of the fear of family repetition than of the desire to be just like them. That is not to say that most daughters do not like their fathers but that they do not want to feel they are destined to find lovers who share their weaknesses. Thus, if their fathers were overly shy and emotionally unavailable most women would consciously want to avoid lovers of that type. The wish behind the fear can be more powerful and, unfortunately for the woman who wants to change, completely unconscious. Thus, if she thinks she wants a demonstrative lover unlike her father, she may end up with one just like him because of the force of his emotional hold over her.

Americans have traditionally been dissatisfied with their childhoods. They have been governed by a dream of the future rather than a desire to repeat the past. Generations in the nineteen-forties and fifties made more money than their parents in order to move to the suburbs and purchase the good things of life. The nineteen-eighties generation frequently have less money than their forebears, but vow to outdo them psychologically by having deeper and more satisfying relationships. They fear being wage slaves like their fathers or victims of empty nests like their mothers. They plan to work and realize their potentials. Before very long our generations will be more like one another as our society matures. We will not think our mothers and fathers did so badly and will be content to emulate them. Some of the adventure of a young society will be gone then but so will much of the strain and anxiety.

Six

CHANGING YOUR FATHER'S EFFECT

Although nowadays there are a confusing number of schools of psychological and psychiatric thought, two major ones of historical importance still exert fundamental influence: the psychoanalytic and the behavioral. The psychoanalytic focus is on the individual's history, the impact of significant life events on the mind, the resistance to remembering sexually and aggressively troubling incidents, and the need to integrate and overcome these dark unconscious forces in order to freely master and enjoy the present. Behaviorism completely ignores the inner workings of the mind. Behavior is viewed as occurring in a specific situation and as something which can be changed or modified through learning. The behaviorist seeks to be scientific and stick to what is observable.

There are difficulties with each approach. The psychoanalytic can become so focused on inner fantasy life that the effect on daily functioning can be neglected. Study of sexual fantasy, for example, can become so consuming that the positive impact on sexual performance is forgotten. The woman may learn about her secret desire for her father but unless she understands how her own genitals work and can communicate this knowledge to her lover her sex life will remain unsatisfactory. Similarly, she may know why she is inhibited in the bedroom, but unless she practices free sexual behavior with the man for whom she cares she is unlikely to become more liberated in her erotic life. The behaviorist approach has its problems also. In spite of the behaviorist's teaching, persuasion, praise, and reward, many individuals remain the same. While part of a person's response to a stimulus such as speech or movement is objectively observable, subjective responses such as thinking and feeling are not. In fact, thinking and feeling are responses to a stimulus which many consider aspects of personality, not behavior. This led Freud to contend that the problem lay in the individual's subjective thoughts and the emotions which were associated with them. He tried to modify current overt behavior by changing the perceptions, thoughts, and feelings which preceded it. By talking to the individual and trying to change the way he or she thought and felt he hoped to change the person's actions. But the psychoanalytic cure is very slow and far from consistently effective.

Theories must be pure in order to advance science, but practitioners faced with people with problems in their offices find they must use both approaches. They try to help individuals change unproductive ways of thinking and feeling but they also focus on overt behavior. The sexual therapies offer an excellent example of the need for both. Pure psychoanalysis concerns itself with feelings and fantasies and the role of the past. It is not so focused on present behavior. Masters and Johnson address themselves to current observa-

ble sexual reality with little or no attention to the inner workings of the mind. Clinicians soon found that this latter approach frequently failed as couples who were instructed to
perform a particular ameliorative sexual exercise did not do
so because of negative feelings toward one another. The inner
workings of their minds had to be considered in order to help
them change their behavior.

Any adverse effect on a woman of thirty years' influence by
her father is so complex that first it requires the analytic understanding of how it altered her thinking and feeling in areas
which trouble her in adulthood, and then she must make the
strong effort to change her unproductive behavior. While
analytic insight often is a necessary prerequisite to behavioral
change it is not invariably so. But most of us cannot change
complicated, repetitive patterns in our lives by simply vowing
to do so. We have to understand what we are facing first and
then try to do something about it.

DISCOVERING WHAT IS REALLY WRONG

A woman has trouble with her lovers. It is a source of pain
and unhappiness. She feels lonely, longing for a man with
whom to share her life. Time and again she is disappointed.
The new exciting love pales, cold angers intervene, and again
she is alone. She wonders what is wrong. Are all men preda-
tors? Is there something wrong with her? She talks to her
friends, to a therapist, but the answer continues to elude her.
She becomes discouraged. It will not be possible for her to
change the pattern unless she knows the full story of how and
why it occurs.

In this case she seeks the warm, exciting, unconditional acceptance of the childhood oasis and cannot adjust to the posi-

tive and negative feelings of adulthood. The crush a new man has on her initially replaces the undivided attention of her father. Then it fades. But she does not know any of this yet. She will have to remember first, tie past and present together, and only then will she be able to begin to change.

Much gets in the way of her understanding. Each new man is different and his ways of hurting her vary. It seems like a string of bad choices rather than anything within herself. If she could only learn to choose better. She resists the notion that she is intolerant to reasonable adult attention, prefers to believe men inconsiderate rather than that she is overly demanding. The idea that her father spoiled her for adult lovers seems foreign. She does not remember any warm oasis to which she desires to return. If anything her father was cold. She believes they talked about school and current events, never about feelings and personal reactions. The good times between father and her are buried and she cannot see how they influence her adult relationships.

It is a psychiatric fact that negative feelings toward loved ones obscure positive ones. Young people complain about their parents much more easily than speak of their love. Spouses readily criticize and must be reminded by therapists, Ann Landers, and the American Association of Florists to express kindness. The positive between people is taken for granted. It is the negative that is noticed. A woman usually talks more readily about her father's absence, drinking, inability to express feelings, or excessive interest in work and money. She complains that he never talked to her about what really mattered but spoke of banalities, that he was excessively reserved and uncomfortable.

Powerful emotions obscure balanced vision and understanding. The recollection of a trauma may blind a daughter to the warmth she shared with her paternal ancestor. As Elvin

Semrad, the beloved teacher of hundreds of Boston psychiatrists, was fond of saying, "As long as people are mad at each other, they can't let each other go. I've never seen anybody get mad at anybody unless he matters to her. I have learned over the years that the only way a father and daughter can part is when they acknowledge how much they love each other. As long as they don't admit this, as long as they 'hate' each other, they stick together like glue. It happens with mothers too."

Why can hate between father and daughter be so adhesive? One would think that a detested individual would be easier to leave. In fact many adolescents look down on their parents unconsciously so it will be less difficult for them to break away from home without excessive longing and sadness. This kind of pure loathing and devaluation of the parent can serve as an aid to separation. But the binding type of hate is the kind arising from an unrecognized wish. The daughter is disappointed in her hope that father will fulfill her needs. To this extent she remains glued to him in the wish that he'll satisfy her. As Leston Havens, M.D., a professor of psychiatry at Harvard Medical School and student of Dr. Semrad, explained, it is her "great expectations" that keep her close.

THE TWO-LIFE-CYCLE MODEL

Strong emotions can blur a woman's view of present problems and to father's role in them. The two-life-cycle model I have proposed will enable you to analyze your life in an orderly way and to gain perspective on father's effect on it. By thinking about your three decades with him in systematic fashion you will be liberated from the extremes of hero worship and angry disappointment. No longer obsessed with his faults nor preoccupied with his good points, you will be able to clearly assess his continuing effect on you. The two-life-cycle model will give you perspective on how his strengths and weaknesses affected you and permit you to maximize the assets you derived from your years with him while minimizing the liabilities.

THEORY OF THE FALL OF FATHER

Because no man can remain an ideal hero forever to his worshipful little girl, every father must fall. The degree and timing of his descent profoundly influence the level of maturity his daughter achieves. Those struggling to remain saints attempt to hold on to and protect adult oasis girls, while the ones who shock or desert leave adolescent-like women prematurely forced into independence yet unable to stand on their own. The timing and severity of father's fall evoke responses ranging from naïveté to compassionate acceptance to shocked insecurity. Men who pretend to be perfect encourage their offspring to remain childlike in their expectations of themselves and others. Those who fall suddenly and excessively, especially when their daughters are too young, can scar them badly, leaving the women afraid to trust men as lovers or at work and with badly shaken self-esteem. The trauma can be overcome, but it takes a long time.

When a man reveals his humanity to his daughter in a gradual and caring way when she is old enough to stand it he actively prepares her for adulthood. By abandoning his role as her hero he aides her in leaving him. By not irretrievably destroying his standing in her eyes he allows her to have confidence to trust others. As she comes slowly to terms with his faults she learns feelings of compassion and acceptance for herself and the men she will meet. In time she realizes that he has made some of the same adjustments in his feelings toward her. He is no longer the only man in her life. She is no longer the chaste worshipful little virgin, but has become a sexual woman who also has faults and limitations. Both father and daughter must get over their disappointments in one another and accept each other realistically. They settle for the realities of life in each other, accompanied by some normal feelings of anger and regret. As the oasis fantasy subsides a woman becomes able to accept human frailties. Her normal anger over father's fall will help her to separate from him during her adolescent years and later. But to become truly mature, a woman must transform that adolescent rage into compassion, open love, and realistic expectations. These qualities are essential in your life and you can learn them through the stages you passed through with your father. This drama will be replayed many times in your life as people who seemed ideal disappoint you. Your ability to accept their shortcomings will enable you to form long-lasting close relationships. Having dealt with the fall of father successfully leaves a deep imprint on every aspect of your life.

In the second decade of a girl's life the relationship with her father changes greatly. The unreality between the little girl's hero and his doll becomes sharply modified. She begins to see his faults (sometimes, even ones he does not have) and he increases his expectations as his love becomes more realistically based and less unconditional. These normal changes are attended by strong feelings on both sides. She doesn't like his rules and criticisms and he doesn't like her disobedience and rebellion. The result is the obvious battles between parent and adolescent child accompanied by sadness over the loss of what once was. When one or the other gets too mad or sad it may lead to withdrawal, which if it becomes permanent can hurt both of them, but especially the developing young woman.

The fall of father, therefore, refers to his loss of status as hero in the oasis of unconditional love and acceptance of childhood. His adolescent daughter begins to see his real strengths and weaknesses as they begin the long process of separation prior to her going out on her own. She sees the real limitations of her middle-aged male parent, that his career is limited, his marriage perhaps troubled, his personality flawed, some of his habits bad. In earlier adolescence, when she discovers his weaknesses or becomes the brunt of his rules and criticisms, she may react with rage and bitterness. Father and daughter may have some very bad fights. Or he may hide in the office or after hours with friends and colleagues, leaving his wife to deal with the difficult adolescent. Toward the end of the teen years the daughter may become more accepting of her father's real shortcomings and less attacking because of disappointment that he has not turned out to be the ideal parent he seemed to be when she was little. Many women require more than the teen years to get over the failure of father's implied promise of childhood—to be perfect, strong, and provide unconditional love. This, of course, is in no way peculiar to women. We all spend our lives recovering from our childhoods.

However painful the experience of the fall of father is for both, it is absolutely crucial to a woman's normal development. It readies her for a real man of her own. There are no unconditionally loving fathers of the oasis period out there in adult life, no perfect men. Learning this during adolescence is easier in many ways than when a woman is in her thirties and forties.

Of course much of the battle is really about separation. Both their hearts are breaking over the loss of the oasis. As

Dr. Semrad said, "Every time you put a mile between a father and a daughter, her heart aches a little." The anger and the fights counteract the sadness and make it more bearable. But unless they abandon the myth of childhood unconditional love and begin to face each other realistically as adults, separation (psychologically more than geographically) will not occur and the girl will not grow into a mature woman.

The fall of father is integrally connected with the building of adult responsibility in the daughter. In childhood she is the perfect little girl and in adolescence she painfully makes the beginning transition to maturity. Not yet ready to accept blame, she says, in effect, "It's not my fault; look at this family."

In this transitional decade from unconditionally loved and accepted girl to responsible adult her self-esteem suddenly drops. Having been fantasy-based in childhood, convinced she could be a star if she wanted, she is suddenly confronted with her limitations and pubescent changes and feels awkward and inept. Through the decade she begins to build her self-esteem on a realistic base, by facing her talents and weaknesses and cultivating skills and mastery. Fathers who are patient, kind, and not too exacting during this difficult time do best. They must be prepared to take a certain amount of abuse.

As the adolescent girl builds her realistically based self-esteem and her skills she is also preparing herself for a career. No longer daddy's little girl, she is becoming a responsible woman capable of functioning in the market place.

Sex is a major factor in the fall. If the first decade takes place in the Garden of Eden, then after the apple is eaten everything becomes different. Father and daughter must somehow cope with her developing womanhood and her recognition that he too is sexual. It is to be remembered that this is occurring during his forties at a time when he may be reevaluating his career and marriage. Sex is an issue for her, him, and them. Some handle it by withdrawal as father hands daughter over to mother. Some fathers become intensely concerned, worry about loss of virginity, or are excessively interested in her body and growing sexual activity. The rare father and daughter accept sexuality in stride. But whether withdrawn, too involved, or accepting, daughter's recognition of father's sexuality and he of hers means the Paradise of Childhood is lost, never again can he be its pure hero, and they must always appear clothed before one another.

As the growing young woman learns to accept and be generous with her fallen father, so she learns to accept her own strengths and weaknesses, to live with herself and with others. When a woman realizes her father is not perfect, that he disappoints her, and when she learns to accept this fact and enjoy him for his strengths, she will have advanced a long way toward her own maturity.

DIAGNOSIS

A woman, therefore, needs to think about the troubled patterns in her life, the failed love affairs, unsatisfying jobs, lack of adult confidence to decide, achieve, and retain what she wants. Then she must understand her father's continuing internal psychological and external ongoing influence on her unhappy habitual behaviors and childish insecurities. The nature of father's fall and its resolution or lack thereof is a good place for a woman to focus in order to understand herself. She will then be able to make a self-diagnosis as to why certain destructive patterns recur in her life.

The word "diagnose" means to distinguish or know, and in

medicine refers to recognizing a disease from its symptoms. More than a mere label, it is the conclusion reached about causation from which therapeutic action is taken. An accurate diagnosis of the subtle, continuing influence of your father is a crucial first step prior to changing destructive patterns. Women whose fathers have adversely affected them in one or more areas of their lives can be divided into two main diagnostic groups: the *arrested* and the *repetitious*. The arrested have never matured, but remain oasis or adolescent girls in some or all aspects of their feelings and behavior throughout their lives. The repetitious destructively duplicate the three stages with father over and over as adults.

ARRESTED

It is the rare woman who regards herself as an immaturely arrested child or adolescent. Usually it is others who see her this way. We experience our immaturities not directly but indirectly. Rare is the woman who thinks, "I am such a spoiled oasis girl that it would have been impossible for anyone to have paid enough attention to me at last night's dinner party." Instead she feels a derivative of this. "My dinner partner was cold and unfriendly. I don't like the way he treated me." Or she may go home from the party feeling depressed and defeated not because she recognizes her excessive need to be the center of attention but because she feels ugly and unloved. Her childlike self-esteem, excessively dependent upon being doted on, is too fragile and she plummets into despair. Some women monopolize attention in a group. If they are good at entertaining they are appreciated and leave happily. People may eventually tire of giving so much to these needy performers who show little interest in others. The oasis star wonders why the invitations have stopped coming, feels hurt, but has no idea of the correct diagnosis: her emotional immaturity. The arrested woman experiences rages and depressions but remains unaware of the true cause of her difficulty. It would help her to overcome the considerable amount of suffering her childishness causes her if she could recognize herself as arrested and if so at what level and in which areas of her life. A full understanding of her relationship to her father will help her do so.

Adult women who have not progressed beyond the oasis level emotionally usually have had too much or too little attention from their fathers when they most needed it. Those who had too little crave it as adults, while those who had too much have never had the chance to grow out of it.

One way to overcome the great difficulty any arrested woman has in self-diagnosis is to think about her father's fall. How and when did it happen and in what way? This will help her gain insight into whether or not she is fixated and at what level. She may have remained an oasis girl or an adolescent. The typical childlike woman's father struggled not to fall at all, but to remain a sexless ideal hero, all powerful and good. He was always there, met all her needs, and in not frustrating her brought up a daughter hardly able to stand disappointment as an adult. Such women remain emotionally united with their male parents all their lives. Because no other lover or employer treats them as well they remain chronically unhappy. They continue to yearn for unconditional love, for that time when they drew and colored a picture of a house with a tree next to it for kindergarten and their father saw it, was delighted, and told them how good it was. His spontaneous exuberance fulfilled a child's normal need. When he told her how pretty she was in her new dress when she was only three he made her smile happily. To be encouraged, loved, made much over, to be told how grown-up, how bright we are, is a normal need of childhood. And all our lives it leaves its mark. We want to be accepted, not criticized. Although we maturely understand that criticism is unavoidable we never really like it, and deep down each and every one of us yearns for that simpler time in the past when we were worshiped just for ourselves. We did not have to do anything and our parents looked at us with love. If we did a little something, drew a picture, did a dance, picked out a tune on the piano, praise was lavished and smiles shown.

It is normal for father and daughter to try to hide faults and even reality from one another in an effort to preserve the oasis. She tries to keep her loss of virginity secret should it happen. Even lesser matters which would excite his disapproval are kept from him by her. He too hides his faults and weaknesses in a Victorian effort to remain the hero in her eyes. He is influenced by the cultural ideal of fatherhood and tries to be a strong, pure symbol of the caretaker and authority figure, not a flesh-and-blood man with weaknesses and vices. She wants him to continue to think of her as special, pure, and perfect. Both fear upsetting and disappointing one another.

It is essential that this normal reluctance to appear realistically to one another be gradually overcome. There is a real danger if *no* fall occurs. The woman will be left a child if daddy pretends to be perfect and succeeds. She will remain unrealistic in her expectations of men, too easily upset and outraged by their treatment of her. She may develop too much basic trust and not enough healthy adult skepticism. While her self-esteem and security will be intact when she is in an oasislike marriage or job, she will remain too dependent on the approval of others.

If a woman's father tried to perpetuate this happy oasis too long and unrealistically he may have made their attachment too tight and hampered her separation and maturation. Since it is very difficult for a woman to be aware of being arrested at a childlike level, thinking about her father's fall may help her deduce this about herself. Is he still your hero? Is there no other man who has been a fraction as kind to you? Did he anticipate your every need and give you anything you asked for? Was he doing so at five, fifteen, and twenty-five? Think about what effect this perfect father may have had on your adulthood. Does any lover have a chance to live up to your father's record? Will any employer ever appreciate your efforts as wholeheartedly?

Your almost perfect father may have bound you emotionally while leaving you free to pursue a career. Thus you may be a busy career woman without a lover. It is possible to be an oasis girl in some areas and not others. Some men encourage competence rather than dependence within the oasis while avoiding the sexual side of the fall. Thus some very successful women executives may speak in glowingly unrealistic terms of their pure hero fathers. These men encouraged the careers of these unmarried, asexual female executives. The price of no fall was paid in their private lives.

There is another kind of father an oasis-arrested woman may have had, not a hero but a villain. Women who have not received their normal quotient of care as children may seek it ever after. About a third of the fathers of the women studied provided too little attention during their daughters' first decade for a variety of reasons including death, divorce, abandonment, working constantly, and being withdrawn at home. Unlike those with a normal or excessive oasis period, these women were quite aware of their deprivation. Many were able to overcome it and form good relationships with men, but all had similar problems.

The scars left by the indifferent or absent father in the first decade of a girl's life show up in relationships with men, in sex, in the ability to deal with work, and in self-confidence in general. Some women have a great deal of difficulty ever warming up to men if they have not had the experience of being stirred up by and in turn captivating their fathers. The excitement they once felt toward them serves as a template for that which is aroused by adult lovers. Having once been a flirt for her paternal parent, dressed to attract him, combed her hair to win his attention, such a woman uses her long-ago-learned wiles on the men in her life.

The woman who has not been stimulated by and in turn enthralled her father as a child is likely to have several problems as an adult which she has to overcome. She will probably feel insecure about attracting men. Another characteristic of these deprived women can be excessive hunger for male attention, of which they can never get enough. At parties they sometimes annoy other women as they grab for stage center and pout when they don't get it. Insatiable hunger for male attention is a somewhat more difficult problem to overcome, especially when it achieves the status of an addiction. A love addict must recognize and admit to herself that she is so afflicted in order to be able to perform the hard job of weaning herself. Finding a good man and staying with him, resisting the desire to have all the others, learning to put up with the quieter delights of a long-term relationship rather than the thrill of captivating new men—all this can be achieved. But there is no easy solution, no words a psychiatrist can say to make the addiction easily, magically overcome. There is only hard work.

Another difficult legacy of the father-ignored woman is her anger at him and at all men. If there is one thing such a woman (it applies to men too) cannot stand it is being ignored. It makes her furious. And fury destroys intimacy and closeness between the sexes. If father-deprived women do not overcome their hostility they end up very lonely. They may believe they are actively looking for a man while not trying at all or keep searching only to have their relationships destroyed by the inevitable angers that arise over the long term. These women don't just get mad and feel ambivalent, they become enraged. Normal angers are magnified by ancient ones. The hope for these women is to become fully conscious of their rage toward the fathers who ignored them and to differentiate these old reactions from those in the present which trigger them. Learning when they are too angry at lovers or spouses for insufficient reason can help them bear and put into perspective these uncomfortable negative feelings, which previously have destroyed or deadened their adult relationships. Calming angers will make them less lonely and miserable with current loved ones.

Women who were father-ignored little girls have trouble in their careers too. They have excessive need for attention and their anger harms work relationships. Their fragile self-esteem can make them too dependent or too upset should they be criticized or make a mistake. Such deprived women also have not had the guidance and support from father that the case histories of the majority of successful females reveal. She has not seen how he operates through his words or firsthand by his actions. The model not there, she will have to learn as an adult for the first time how to manage herself in business, unless she has had the benefit of other male sources of support and guidance while growing up, including older brothers, uncles, teachers, friends of the family, and boyfriends. Overcoming the absence of male support and models in childhood can certainly be successfully accomplished and many women have been able to do so.

ARRESTED IN ADOLESCENCE

While the oasis girl is most likely to have had an overly devoted or absent father, one who struggled not to fall at all or who did so in the first ten years of her life, the adolescence-arrested woman usually has had a father who fell excessively in her teens. There are many kinds of severe shocks a male parent can give his adolescent daughter. He can die, desert, become chronically ill, be fired, abuse alcohol, be promiscuous, and abruptly lose the status of hero. The oasis is not only lost, it is poisoned, and the effects on his daughter are profound.

As the pendulum has swung historically from a Victorian to a Narcissistic Age the incidence of the excessive fall increases while that of the no fall declines. The climbing divorce rate is one reason. This failure to live up to the cultural ideal of Fatherhood is painful to fathers as well as to their daughters. Deep guilts and sadnesses exist because of the inability to live up to the accepted norm. It is having a powerful effect on the lives of young women and in their willingness to trust and relate to men.

A severely scarred woman who has not gotten over the desertion, drunkenness, failure, or weakness of her father will have great trouble trusting men. The psychological trauma will make her avoid men, seek only ones she can control completely, or suffer a series of endings and disappointments as she contemptuously discovers the weaknesses in her latest lover. Fortunately, humans are strong and flexible and able to overcome the experience of the excessive fall of a parent. The excessive fall of father can shake a daughter's self-esteem and harm her career by making it difficult for her to relate to male colleagues and mentors. She may be left mistrustful and tentative, unable to commit herself to her work, perhaps feeling her efforts will not be rewarded, that all will turn out badly as it did with her father.

The excessive fall of father in the teen years strikes a woman at a time when she is trying to separate from him. Normally to do so she is rebellious and angry and needs a strong male parent to react against. When he suddenly proves weak or, worse still, absent, her process of separation is arrested. She is left neither independent nor dependent but vacillates between the two. She becomes the kind of person who cannot take direction yet is unable to proceed without it. Because she remains adolescent in her inability to reliably control her anger and sex drive she impulsively fights with her boss or sleeps with him. Her relationships are stormy.

Like the oasis-stuck girl, she too is unaware that it is her adolescent immaturity that is responsible for the chaotic quality of her career and love affairs. But if a woman is chronically unhappy she might think about when and how severe was the fall of her father and its effect on her development. Understanding that it left her angry and unsupported will give her insight into how to begin building herself to overcome this trauma. The knowledge that it is not the boss she is furious with but her father will help her begin to do better in her career. Similarly, the realization that her anger at her employer stems from her unwillingness to take direction yet inability to self-motivate will enable her to progress. Because she is neither adult nor child, but like a teenager back and forth between the two, her life is in turmoil. Her father's influence and his excessive fall has contributed greatly to her misery. To overcome it she must gain insight into his continuing adverse effect upon her.

REPETITION

These women are not arrested but repeat the stages of development with father blindly and destructively. The reason is that they are in conflict about each stage of development. With men, for example, they delight in the oasis of a new relationship, the lavished attention and special qualities of a new crush. But soon the conflict begins. They delight in being little girls but they also do *not* want to be immature. They feel stifled and childlike and want to do something more with themselves. The relationship with the new lover progresses to the stormy stage of adolescence, sexy and romantic but filled with struggles over dependence and independence. They want to be together yet when in each other's company they long for freedom. They wish to make their own decisions yet are afraid to do so. The relationships grow progressively unpleasant as the woman longs for maturity and independence. She wants to enjoy her lover as an adult, independent woman, to unite with him in strength and self-confidence not in need and uncertainty. Her union achieves adult level for a time. She is pleased and proud but because she is in conflict about being grown up she begins to develop negative emotions, to feel lonely and neglected, and to desire the special glow of the oasis once again. Her "mature" relationship dissolves and she searches the beginning of the next one.

Not all repetition of the stages with father is self-destructive. As described in the chapter on careers, the ability to journey again from oasis to adult is essential to a woman's successful climb in a business organization. But in sex and relationships this pattern can be very debilitating as one promising liaison after another ends in unhappiness.

While conflict is normal in all of us, the blind repeaters of the developmental stages with father have too much of it. We all desire the unconditional love of the oasis deep down, but these women want it so much they keep searching for it, while at the same time they reject it and feel stifled by it. They look for the father-hero of the little girl, the falling father of adolescence, and the parental companion of maturity. But because they have never successfully completed these stages they keep returning to them.

This group of women have a somewhat easier time of breaking their unhappy patterns than do those who are arrested. They find immaturity unsatisfying and continually strive to grow. The arrested are more likely to blame others and not accept responsibility for the trouble in their lives. Once a woman sees her difficulty as originating within herself she is more ready and able to overcome it.

The type of repetitious pattern described here may help explain part of the current fashion of serial monogamy. With the increasing number of excessive-fall fathers associated with the increasing divorce rate and the narcissistic generation, more daughters are unable to successfully complete their cycle of development with him and are left scarred. Thus their longing for the warmth of the original oasis before his fall draws them into a continual search. But if the timing and severity of his fall were not too great these women were given enough by him so as not to have become arrested. Thus they find the rediscovered oasis too childish and want to enjoy the mastery and competence of adulthood. But the wound is great enough to weaken them and draw them back to the special, unconditional love of their early years.

In order to interrupt this heartbreaking repetition these women must diminish the conflict within them. One way is by coming to terms with father's adverse influence on their lives.

A second is by putting his fall into perspective and accepting it. By coming to a reconciliation with him in her mind and heart she will be able to begin to free herself of destructive patterns in her life.

RECONCILIATION

From age twenty onward a woman discovers her real father. Not the hero of childhood or the antihero of adolescence; she sees the man. When a woman recognizes that her father isn't perfect but nevertheless has a lot of strengths she is well along toward maturity. The discovery permits her to be realistic in her relationship to others and to begin to have normal expectations of herself. A daughter of a perfect man would have the problem of living up to his impossible level. Landing on her feet after his fall, she can continue to enjoy his assets and forgive or ignore his weaknesses. Mutual respect, affection, and commonality of interest between them allow maintenance of meaningful ties. She can benefit from his experience, support, and caring while he continues to be enlivened by her youth and enthusiasm. The generations have a lot to give and take from each other. She keeps him young and he keeps her anchored. Accepting his weaknesses and enjoying his strengths, she becomes strong and independent yet able to draw on the positive aspects of their continuing relationship both inwardly and in fact.

By taking her feelings for her father, separating them from him, and putting them into herself, a woman takes the final step toward independence and maturity. She carries out his traditions as he lives on through her, even after his death. Women are a composite of their parents. From their fathers they have traditionally gotten their career strengths and assertiveness. In the future this will undoubtedly be less sex-linked and mothers will contribute much more to their daughters' worldly capacities for thinking and self-respect.

But the more a daughter likes and admires her father, the more she can rid herself of the excessive force of her anger over his weaknesses and capitalize on the positives, the more strength will be in her. She will be able to like the part of herself that is like him and reject the inherited similarities she dislikes.

In reconciliation there is the ability to tolerate ambivalence. The anger of her disappointment over his failures as a parent obscured her deeper love. The two-life-cycle approach helps a woman find balance in the years with father and ultimately within herself. Her full knowledge and acceptance of the mix of her positive and negative feelings toward father helps a daughter to leave him emotionally, not just by physically departing the parental home, but by absorbing his strengths for her own use and rejecting his weaknesses.

She learns to accept her deep longing for his unconditional love. She realizes we all long for the unconditional love of our parents all our lives. It is a yearning from the depths of the heart for unconditional love, the time in each of our lives when we were special, when the parental eye twinkled with delight whenever it watched us. No eye shines more brightly than that of a father for his little daughter and hers for him. The pleasure they give one another has very little of the ambivalence present in most other human relationships.

If many girls have experienced this delightful interlude with father and if the stamp is so deep and indelible that traces can be found even in the oldest, then every woman would benefit from recognizing how the legacy of the childhood oasis influences her throughout her whole life. If there is one universal truth found in the many women I have studied, it is that *no man will love you as your father did when you were a child.* The grown female would do well to be conscious of this fact of life so she can cope with it effectively.

There is, therefore, an extreme paradox in every woman's life. Her model for relationships with men is the one she enjoyed with her father, but her experience will be completely different because no man will ever treat her as well as he did. Lovers and husbands never give unconditional love. They are demanding and have expectations. The more she understands and accepts this the better her chances will be of finding a good adult relationship with a man.

But she will be affected in her career too, if she seeks the adulation father gave her in childhood. A boss is not overcome with delight and effusive with praise every time a woman makes a bright comment in a meeting. How she deals with the gap between her longing for the oasis with father and the realities of her boss's seeming indifference by comparison or outright criticism can deeply affect her career. Once a woman loses her nostalgia for childhood, quiets her adolescent anger, and faces her father realistically, she is able to maturely relate to lovers, her own psyche, and her career. But for a woman either arrested or repeating unhappy patterns the problem is how to change and become mature.

CHANGE

Once a woman has fully analyzed her relationship to her father, using the two-life-cycle approach to achieve balanced understanding, she has the necessary prerequisite for change —insight—but change is never automatic; it requires effort. What drives any person to want to change is suffering. The pain of repeated unhappy love affairs, unsatisfying sexual relations, insecurity, career failures, forces the wish to alter patterns. Recognition of the cause of the discomfort is followed by the knowledge that the woman herself has some control over what happens to her. If there are indeed no good men around then a woman can do nothing about it. But her desperation does not derive from the necessity of factors beyond her control; it is within her power to change. She has the freedom to approach her life differently.

By recognizing alternative ways to behave and feeling the power to make a choice, she then strives to do something differently. Her insight tells her where she is, how she got there, and where she wants to go. She now realizes the power and desire to help herself. The first steps are small. She feels awkward and uncertain but proceeds. She may suffer some failures, but pushes on nonetheless. Soon some successes come. They allow her to dare try more.

She realizes action is required and applies her will and effort. It takes a long time and she does not expect immediate results. Overcoming old habits makes for anxiety. She uses her will, mind, and heart and is willing to feel afraid. She may have to pretend to be sure of herself long before she really has confidence. She acts as though she were able to master a new job before she really feels certain.

She goes against her fears, tries to overcome her negative emotions and to accept responsibility. It is not easy and at times she feels frightened and defeated, but she has made a pact with herself. She knows what she has to do and has vowed nothing will stop her. Her rewards will be greater fulfillment enhancing the value of her life.